The God Session

Healing the Past and Embracing the Future with Scripture, Science, and Energy Medicine

Kathryn Springman

I have tried to recreate events, locales, and conversations from my memories of them. In order to maintain their anonymity, I have omitted or changed the names of individuals. I also may have changed some identifying characteristics and details, such as physical properties, occupations, locations, and places of residence.

The information contained within this book is strictly for educational purposes. This book is not intended as a substitute for the medical advice of physicians. The reader should regularly consult a physician in matters relating to his/her health, and particularly with respect to any symptoms that may require diagnosis or medical attention.

Every BODY Tells a Story ™
Trademark Kathryn Springman

Cover Design Lissie Teehee,
Lissie@LissieTeehee.com,
Photo © Thinkstock Photos

Book design and production by Angelique Mroczka,

www.authorgeek.com

Editing by Matt Rott, Rott Enterprises,

mattrottediting@gmail.com

Diagram illustrations by Kathryn Springman,
Images © Thinkstock Photos

Bonus Material illustrations by Ben Jenkins,
www.bjenk.com

Author portrait by Steffanie Halley,
www.SteffanieHalley.com

ISBN 10: 0-9971889-0-1
ISBN 13: 978-0-9971889-0-5

Download the Free Bonus Materials!

Success is easier when you do the exercises on your own worksheets. By using these bonus materials, you can make your own notes and follow along step-by-step throughout each section of the book. Feel free to take these materials along with you so you have them whenever you need them.

Go to www.KathrynSpringman.com to download your free copy!

To those who seek the Truth,
may you be blessed when you find it and embrace it.

To those who have wished for healing
but didn't know how or where to start,
may your journey to health
begin here.

Contents

Acknowledgements

To God, who wrote the book of my life and who partners with me to help me stay on the right page, in the right paragraph, and on the right word—and who counsels me, guides me, and nurtures me every step of the way.

To the visiting pastor who preached on the story of the woman who was to be stoned (John 7:53-8:11). In that sermon, he encouraged us to look at not only that story, but every story from multiple perspectives. "Look at the story from the eyes of each person involved. What insights do you gain from those perspectives?" From that moment on, I have endeavored to do this not only when reading, but in life. To this pastor I say thank you. No words can express the depth of this gift in my life.

At one of the most difficult times in my life, a friend introduced me to BodyTalk. Throughout my training, scriptures would come to mind and I would begin to make the connection: "Oh, that's why the Bible says that!" I sat under great instructors who taught me more about perspectives—not from what is going on "out there," in the external world but what is going on "in here," within the internal world and how they are the same.

To John Veltheim, founder of The BodyTalk System™ and Mindscape™, and Esther Veltheim for her

BreakThrough System, I express my deep and unfailing gratitude for the gift you have given to the world and to me. Hearts are touched and lives are changed. Mine is only one of many.

With BodyTalk, I learned that Every BODY Tells a Story™ and that we only need to listen in order to understand the best way to find balance. Mindscape increased my ability to trust my intuition. BreakThrough taught me that we only need to observe what is in our own environments to know what we need in our lives. And that rather than blaming others, we must first look within and take responsibility for our own thoughts, feelings, and behaviors. This is by far one of the best systems to help people get out of the victim mentality and learn to walk forward and lead victorious lives.

Among those who forged the way ahead for us: Thank you, Charles Kraft, for your ministry in deliverance, deep wound healing, and spiritual warfare. Thank you, Arthur Burk, for your insights in spiritual warfare, the seven curses, nurturing the spirit, spiritual gifts, time and land, and fractals, among a myriad of other spiritual concepts. Thank you Megan Caldecourt for giving further insight into Arthur Burk's concepts.

Many, many thanks to Crystal, friend and practitioner extraordinaire, who listened while I unleashed my ideas, and, as enthusiastically as I, put them into practice. To her children, thank you for sharing your ideas and your mother. You, too, are extraordinary and highly gifted. I love you all.

To my friend who introduced me to BodyTalk: You know who you are, and while I honor your wish to remain anonymous, I wish to acknowledge you. Thank you for the introduction. Thank you for letting me practice my new skills and allowing me to think aloud. For where I am today . . . it's all your fault! :) I love you.

To my father, a brilliant and gifted pioneer in the medical field whose bedside manner both calms and reassures, and whose hard work, humility, and compassion are unsurpassed: I love you.

To my sister who said to me, "Don't you think it's about time to write that book?" Thank you for calling me out. This project wouldn't have gotten out of the thinking-about-doing-it-one-day stage without you. Thank you for being one of my biggest fans. As I said to my friend, I say to you . . . it's all your fault! :) I love you.

To my husband and children, you have been with me every step of the way in this journey of life, and we've learned much together. I love each of you, and pray for you, thanking God that you are a part of my life.

Last, but not least, thank you to family and friends who encouraged me along the way, and to my clients who allowed me to be a part of their healing journey. What a privilege that is!

From the Author

I wish I had known this information a long time ago. I wish they taught it in church. But our journeys are our journeys. We discover all we need at the right time and in the right place. It means more to us that way. Since necessity is the best teacher, we learn information faster at exactly the moment it is needed. Maybe we heard it before, maybe not. Or maybe, in the hearing, it felt more like an overload that we weren't ready for, so it just didn't have a place to land.

Some of what I will tell you will be welcome like a gentle rain on a hot summer day. Some of what I will tell you may have you screeching at me. If this happens, you may be like me—someone who fought against what she could not explain or control until there was no choice but to examine it with a prayer in her heart to say, "If this is true, let it be glaringly obvious. If this is false, let it also be obvious, and let the falsehoods fall away, never to return."

The nice thing about writing a book is that we get to tell our stories and give information that we feel will benefit others. Most of what I lay before you is from my experience personally, and in clinic as a BodyTalk practitioner. The nice thing about reading a book is that you can find the parts that work for you. You can lay the rest aside and come back to it later. This book will be a kind friend that will call to you when you really need it, and continue to be a resource for you. Sometimes, you may need to set it aside so that you can process the information, research it for yourselves, and see how it fits in your life. Some of you will need to do that, some won't.

Early on in my energy healing journey, a friend of mine reminded me that there are really only two sources of energy in the world. Some of my Christian mentors would comment that for everything God has, Satan has a counterfeit. Taking that a step further, my friend often says, "God good. Devil bad." It's her way of saying, "Where is the source?"

This book lays down concepts that are both simple and complex at the same time. Together we will explore not only the scientific but also the energetic and spiritual principles. I am not a scientist, nor an expert in these fields. My expertise is in encouraging the innate ability of the body to heal. I was born to move energy. I have lived and breathed this information most of my life, and have applied it to a professional practice for the past eight years.

Prior to learning any alternative healing modalities, like BodyTalk and other energy healing techniques, I trained in intercession and spiritual warfare. Intercession is probably best described as praying or "standing in the gap." Then, after I started my BodyTalk practice, I endeavored to learn more, and began to develop new techniques to augment my clinical practice. In any given session that I facilitate, we may use BodyTalk, spiritual warfare, or any of the techniques that we will explore in this book—techniques that you will learn so that you can experience healing in your life.

Everyone can benefit from the information and techniques in this book, even though it is intended to aid Christians in understanding energy medicine concepts. By blending science with ancient biblical wisdom to undergird those principles, we will explore those biblical truths that merge everything together into an exciting journey that unveils the awesomeness of who we are and who we were created to be.

You may find that you disagree with some of the things I have written—and that's ok. At anytime, if you feel that I am off the mark, then I ask that you pray this prayer for me: "Lord, please let her always see your truth—not my truth, not her truth, but the unvarnished divine truth that comes only from you."

Introduction

Have you tried and tried to receive healing in a particular area of your life, yet no matter what the healing just has not come? Do you feel as though there are obstacles at every turn? Wouldn't it be nice to move beyond the obstacles and receive healing, not only for you, but for your family? And even beyond now, to receive healing for future generations?

So many Christians today are struggling with health issues, even though Scripture plainly says, "Beloved, I pray that you may prosper in all things and be in health, just as your soul prospers" (3 John 2 NKJV). While it is evident that this is His plan for us, it is not always easy to attain it. In the pages to come, we will combine Scripture, science, and new explanations of energy medicine to explore various obstacles that block our way to whole health. We will explore techniques to help heal our wounds, clear our memories and traumas, and release the emotional upheavals. We will find new balance for our spirits, minds, wills, emotions, souls, and bodies.

With over 30 years experience in prayer, intercession, and spiritual warfare, along with 8 years in the energy medicine field, I am pleased to bring you new insights based on the ancient wisdom of God. I believe health is more than what we see in the body. I know that if we are struggling in the health of even one area of our lives— spiritually, mentally, emotionally, or physically—then on some level we are struggling with the health of all. We may observe it more readily in one area, but all areas are affected. Therefore, my approach to health is one that balances all aspects of our being. I believe in miracles, and because I believe in miracles, I am privileged to observe countless breakthroughs in my life and the lives of my family and clients.

There Is No Box With God

Isn't it easier sometimes to organize our lives by putting everything into neat boxes? Then we can find what we want when we want it. Have you noticed there are some things that just won't fit into a box? No matter how hard we try, they just cannot be contained. It is the same with our concepts of God. We try to take all we know and pack it into a box, then say, "That is God." But then we discover that there are some things that just won't fit into that box, because God cannot fit into a box. He challenges us to believe what He says, even though others have told us it is impossible. All things are possible if only we choose to believe.

You Can Ask God Anything.

You have not because you ask not (James 4:2).

In my early 20s, I was attending a prayer meeting during which we received a prayer request from the family of a police officer who had been shot in the back. When we broke into smaller groups, we each took turns praying over the requests we had received, including this one. When it came my turn to pray, I asked God to heal this man so completely that it would be as though it never happened. When I opened my eyes and looked up, the entire group—to a person—were all staring at me in shock. I thought at first that I had done something wrong, but I knew in my heart that it was the right thing to pray. In fact, He tells us that we have not because we ask not. So why not ask? Why wouldn't God want us to be healed completely? I knew this: If I didn't ask, He couldn't say no—but He also couldn't say yes.

Recently, a fellow practitioner reviewed the manuscript for this book and said that even though she has been doing this work for a long time, she found issues coming to mind that needed to be cleared. "I think it's going to be very powerful. I was shifting a lot while reading it, and none of it was new information. It's all the things we tell our clients. It's crazy how simple the message is, but so so so powerful, especially to people who have not been exposed to this before."

The information in the pages to follow is what I share with my clients on a regular basis. The exercises have proven transformational for those who have done them. I can promise that if you read each section and follow the exercises, you will begin to feel a healing that is deeply profound. Each section and each exercise builds on the one before. Healing continues even after you have completed the exercises. You will find new ways of thinking about prayer and new ways to think about health. Let's begin the journey to new and even better spiritual, mental, emotional, and physical health today.

Section 1

Permissions

I'd like to start by telling you a story. Not that long ago, my son and I were in the car. I was driving, and my intention was to turn left at the next major light. Now, this road had a center turn lane that went down the length of the road. A woman pulled out from one of the businesses on the side of the road and was hanging in the middle of this turn lane. Her car was blocking my ability to move into the lane so that I could turn at the next major light. I typically don't react or get upset in traffic situations, because I'm aware that I probably do quite a few things to irritate other drivers. Not that that's my intention, but it is what it is.

In this particular case, I said, "OK lady, you need to move now." I wasn't upset—it was just a statement of fact. Of course, this woman couldn't hear me, but I needed to be able to express it. My son turned to me and said, "You know that you don't have your turn signal on." I said, "That's a true statement." He said, "You don't have your turn signal on a lot." I said, "Also a true statement." He said, "You know, when you don't use your turn signal, you tell everyone around you that they have no right to know where you are going, or to be safe when you are around." My mind translated this as, "You know, when you don't use your turn signal, you give people permission to not know what you want, or where you want to go." I said, "Wow. That's a true statement." He said, "I'll admit that she was the one who was doing something illegal." I said, "Yes, also true." Then he said, "If you'd had your turn signal on, she would've at least known what your intentions were." I said, "That's also true."

Within the context of healing, and before this moment, I would explain permissions as addressing any resistance to healing. It is interesting, then, to think that by not using turn signals we are giving others permission to create obstacles on our road to healing. In other words, permissions (giving authority to do or be something) are a lot like turn signals. I knew that this experience in the car with my son was a divine moment given to me to impart "turn signal" wisdom. It was such a profound moment so of course it is no surprise that I experienced it while I was preparing to write this book.

Prior to the writing phase of the book, I'd been contemplating the permissions topic for some time. Since permissions are integrated into the BodyTalk protocol, I began thinking of all the sessions in which I had seen rapid and life-changing results. In truth, I've been contemplating permissions for the past eight years.

So in that divine moment, I received a new revelation regarding permissions, and that is:

"Permissions are like turn signals."

Proverbs 4:25-26 Let your eyes look straight ahead, and your eyelids look right before you. Ponder the path of your feet, and let all your ways be established.

The Hebrew translation of "established" means "reliable, rested." You look directly ahead at your path; you know where you are going. In this way—letting your path be established—you allow yourself to be able to rest, to set in order, to be steady, steadfast, and strengthened. Through permissions, we turn on our turn signals to rest in and strengthen our paths. God doesn't say we need turn signals, because He makes our paths straight in Him. But *we* need the ability to remove the veil of resistance so that we can see which path to take. In the same way that we use turn signals on our physical roads, we can use permission turn signals on our spiritual paths.

Permissions include the honesty needed to use our turn signals that say, "I'm looking ahead at my path, and it goes that way." God is quick to show us the way when we are willing to give ourselves permission.

When you gaze straight ahead and you know where you're going—and your path is fixed straight in front of you—then you can see that path clearly so you know where you are going. However, sometimes the path is encased in fog and nothing is clear. It takes a tremendous amount of trust to put one foot in front of the other if the path seems obscured. Thus, we may only know a general direction, because when the path is fogged, it similar to having no GPS to guide us.

Permissions give us an ability to make choices and get to our destinations, and allow not only us but everyone else to know our general direction. Even if we're not clear of the exact road to take, we know the end destination. We know where we want to go.

Why do we need to give ourselves permission? Besides knowing where we want to go and establishing that path, we give permission in order to create a solid ground over which to sojourn. In other words, to create a platform for success. It is as though permissions allow us to move through life with ease while giving others permission to know what is that we want in life. The journey becomes a partnership with ourselves, with God, and with others, making our paths and journeys of personal and spiritual growth to better health and better lives much smoother.

I encourage you to give yourself permission to make choices, and to be able to say, "I give myself permission. I choose." The first step? Know what it is that you choose, and, as I'll talk about more later, "own" those choices. In other words, when you make a choice, know why you made it. Do it on purpose, and do it with purpose. Doing something on purpose says, "This is what I plan to do." Doing it with purpose says, "This is why I want to do it." Do it with intention and attention. Give it the attention it deserves, and then set your intentions to follow it through. Your permission turn signals help you set those clear intentions.

Let's think back to those foggy roads. This is where we need to understand a concept about acknowledging our doubts. In Kishori Aird's book, *Essence*, there is a great example that says, "When we at least acknowledge our doubt, we're not polarizing it." We cannot spend so much time in our doubt that we are paralyzed and unable to move forward.

Doubts are there for a very good reason. Doubt asks you to recheck your roadmap or turn on the GPS. Doubt asks you to make sure that you are indeed on the right road. Doubt is your double-check. It is there to ensure that you do know where you're going; that you are doing something on purpose, with purpose. That's the good reason we have doubt. However, when out of balance, doubt is rooted in fear. Fear can paralyze us in our journeys.

If only for ourselves, we need to be able to acknowledge these doubts along our path. By acknowledging doubt, we are saying, "I see you. I recognize you. I acknowledge you." This is similar to how our children (especially small children) sometimes call to us, "Mom, Mom, Mom, Mom," until we finally acknowledge them. When we are willing to at least acknowledge doubt, it does not continue to get even louder and interrupt everything. This is what I call the "I see you" effect. "I see you. I acknowledge you, but I'm not willing to let doubt throw temper tantrums. I take authority over that doubt."

Kishori Aird adds the phrase, "Even if I don't know how." In this, we're saying, "I'm choosing to move down this path, even if I don't know how. I'm making this choice. I know this is what I want, but I may not know exactly how to get there. Even if I don't know how, I know that this is the general direction that I need to take." Here is a very powerful phrase to add to your language: "Even if I don't know how."

I give myself permission to believe.

For several years, I've felt the nudge to write a book. I admit that writing is not my favorite activity. I really would have liked to be able to toss this idea in the "fanciful thinking" pile. But the more that I tried to avoid it, the stronger and more apparent it became that I truly was supposed to do this—to take on this project. I knew that what I had to tell people was true. I say these truths to my clients every day. I knew I needed to extend this information out beyond my client base and into the general public. I knew everything that I'm writing about to be true, not only because I've experienced it myself, but because my clients have experienced it as well. This information is truly transformational. But even knowing that, in came the doubts. "Am I really supposed to write the book? Does God really want me to write the book? Am I really called to write the book? Do I really have something to say? Isn't this old information? Aren't there thousands of other books out there that already say this?"

Then, one morning, I woke up with this phrase in my head: "I give myself permission to believe." Personally, at that time, I needed my own miracle of knowing that I was on the right path. I needed to know that my path was straight. I knew everything was true. I knew I would be establishing bold concepts, but hadn't yet found the research that I knew would support those concepts.

Mark 9:23–24 tells the story about a man whose child needed deliverance. In that story, Jesus said, "Everything is possible for one who believes." Immediately, the boy's father exclaimed, "I do believe! Help my unbelief." Another translation says, "Help me overcome my unbelief." Now, I've heard those scriptures before, and I have given a lot of thought to them. But when I added this together with the phrase "Even if I don't know how," the conversation changed in my mind. I now see the story unfold this way: The father says, "I do believe, help my unbelief." In my mind, I hear him thinking, "Well, okay, I want to believe. I recognize I have doubts, but I just don't know how to get past them. I really need you to help my unbelief. Here are my doubts, but if you could just help me anyway. I want to believe. I want to believe so badly." Jesus honored that. This is where acknowledging our doubts can be so powerful.

Everything came into clear focus for me when I woke up that morning thinking, "I give myself permission to believe. I believe, Lord. Help my unbelief. I believe. I want to believe. I recognize I have doubts, but I choose to believe even if I don't know how. I choose to believe that the message rings true. I choose to believe that this book is a blessing. I choose to believe everything that God has told me about writing the book." Hearing "I give myself permission to believe" gave me the ability to overcome my doubts.

Permissions for Mind, Body, and Emotions

There are many areas where we can give ourselves permission, not the least of which is in spiritual matters. But there are three main areas we will focus on in this section. Remember that permissions can help give us direction. When we get bogged down or stuck somewhere, we need to look at the path we are on. Once we look at the path, how do we give ourselves permission to move beyond where we are, and into a new level of awareness and healing? It can be difficult to recognize which area needs permission. In that case, I say, "I give myself permission (mental, physical, emotional, spiritual)."

Mental Permissions

Mental, physical, and emotional permissions all intermingle together. If we have a physical ailment that we really need and want to be healed, we must think about that first. We need to put some attention toward what we want so we can intentionally move forward. Often though, we need to come to a clear understanding of our definition of "health." Thinking about it now, what is your definition of health? What does that really mean for you? You may say, "Health? Everybody knows what that means." That may be true. But if you aren't sure, it may help to give yourself permission to think through the definition of health, or even "whole health." What does it mean to be something other than a disease?

Let's look at some phrasing choices for someone with diabetes: "I have diabetes" or "I am a diabetic." The phrase "I have" indicates that if you have it, then you can let go of it. It indicates the ability to move beyond it. The phrase "I am" indicates a state of being. How often do you introduce yourself by saying, "Hi, I am _____." The phrase "I am" describes essence. Hence, permission could sound like this: "I give myself permission to redefine what it means to be healthy." "I give myself permission to rethink the way I phrase my state of health." "It is ok for me to state what I observe about my health."

As we begin to think through that, we can begin to see other areas for mental permissions. "I give my mind permission to heal." "It is okay to overcome (my obstacles to whole health)." "It is okay to relax." "It is okay to say what I think." "It is okay to express my wants, my needs, and my concerns."

Physical Permissions

For some, it is possible to use the mental list for the physical. "I give my body permission to sleep (or to be awake)." "It is ok to allow my DNA to change." "I give myself permission to listen to what my body is telling me." "It is ok to appreciate my body, and all it does for me."

The list could go on and on. One of the biggest obstacles to healing is that we are so accustomed to having a *condition*, whether it is some type of pain, headaches, or disease. Often we have had it for so long that we don't know what life would look like without it. The inner voice says, "If I don't have headaches (if I'm not in pain), what else would I talk about?" "If I don't have these allergies, well, what does that mean?" "Doesn't getting old also mean being sick and in pain?"

"I give my body permission to heal (to heal quickly, to heal completely)." "I give myself permission to move through life with the freedom that true health provides me." "I give my body permission to age gracefully while feeling whole and well." "I give myself permission to be freed from inherited predispositions."

Emotional Permissions

You can see that mental and physical permissions begin to intermingle. It is also apparent that there can be a lot of emotion tied up in some of these statements. "How do I *feel* about not being in pain anymore?" Some people receive quite a lot of attention and recognition for being sick. The inner voice may cry, "What does life look like without this disease? How else will I get attention?"

"Better the devil you know than the devil you don't." Maybe not.

It is very probable that we can be very emotionally invested in the pain, sickness, or condition because it brings a level of attention that we may not feel that we would receive otherwise. People feel sorry for us when we are sick. They have more empathy towards us, because there is pain. But what if there is no pain? What if there is no sickness or condition? What if we could be free from that? What does that new dynamic look like? Would we get the same attention?

It can be a scary thought, especially if we think that this is a way for us to receive love and attention. Sometimes it is so scary, that we would rather stay sick. The inner voice says, "I may not like being sick, but at least I know what to expect."

This thought process creates a big emotional investment in staying sick or not getting well. It's not necessarily a healthy emotional investment, but it is an emotional investment. It takes a lot of courage to determine that we really do want that physical health enough that we are willing to face the path that seems to be encased in a dense fog.

Emotional permission statements can sound similar to mental and physical statements, but can also be very different. "I give my emotions permissions to heal. I give my emotional self permission to heal." If you were raised to believe that expressing emotion is a bad thing, then this statement may help: "I give myself permission to express my emotions." "I give myself permission to be my own intrinsic, authentic self. To appreciate and/or express my intrinsic value." "It is ok to release negative emotions." "It is ok to feel positive emotions." "It is ok to love and be loved."

Emotional permissions is a very interesting concept. Do we give ourselves permission not only to feel, but also to release negative emotions and embrace positive ones? First, we need to be able to recognize those negative emotions—or perhaps give ourselves permission to feel them so we can then release them. Then decide what positive emotions counter the negative and embrace those positive emotions.

The Grieving Wife

Early on in my career, I did a session for a woman whose husband had passed away a few years earlier. Even though he had been gone for a few years, she really couldn't get past the grief. In fact, the grief was overwhelming her to the point that she was still feeling it with the same intensity as when he first passed on. What the session revealed was that she had not given herself permission <u>to want</u> to grieve. This was very intriguing for both of us to think about. She needed to say the permission statement, "I give myself permission to want to grieve." Once she was able to <u>want</u> to grieve then, she could give herself permission to actually grieve. Then, she could finally, fully move through her grieving process.

This session was so profoundly moving for her that she felt it through her entire being. Later she told me that she went home, got in the hot tub, and decided to have "a permission party." She sat in the hot tub and said, "I wonder what else I have not given myself permission for?" During her permission party, she thought through different areas of her life and addressed each of them one at a time. She gave herself permission to move through life and to move past the obstacles that had been in her way for so very long.

What is next for you? Some of you have already started giving yourself permission and have begun to think about what this means for you. You may have already started putting words to your permission statement. Some of you have not. Maybe you wonder where to start.

As we move forward, I want you to think about where in your life you feel there is a block or an obstacle, or a detour even. While roadblocks make the road impassable without clearly defining an alternate route, and obstacles may slow you down but can be navigated or circumvented, I would like to note that detours could be God's way of saying, "It is ok to take the scenic route."

Begin to look at where you have not given yourself permission. Maybe you need to give yourself permission for something very specific. Or maybe you need to give yourself permission to take a detour, to take the scenic route.

It is OK to take the scenic route.

One day I was at the health food store where my friend works. A young lady came in and started talking to my friend, who called me over, saying, "Come talk to this lady." During the course of our conversation, the woman told me that she was not sleeping very well. She was waking up at the same time every night. I could tell by the hour that she was waking that the sleeping issues could easily relate to activities of planning and organizing. To double-check and be clear, I asked, "Are you in the middle of a lot of planning and organizing?" "Oh, yes," she said, "I'm getting out of the military in two weeks and I really want to go into video game design. It's my passion. In fact, I have a game I have been working on for several years." I said, "Okay." She said, "Well, but I have a problem." I said, "What is that?" She said, "Well, where I really want to go to school is in this particular town. It's quite a ways away, and it's an expensive school. I just don't have the funds for it right now." I said, "Okay." She said, "There is an alternative. There is another school where I could start, but it's not where I want to end up."

I then asked, "Have you thought about giving yourself permission to take the scenic route? That it's okay to take a detour? Have you thought that by going to the first school that you know that you can afford, you can further develop the game you are working on—especially since it's the game of your dreams? While you are working on it, you can use it in some of your assignments so you can get feedback from your teachers. You can finish the game and use it as a learning experience during your development stage. Use it as a growing experience. Then, take what you have learned in the interim school and transfer to the other school that you want to be the final destination in your schooling. Then, use that as your final project. In the meantime, you'll be learning all along the way. It's the scenic route for the destination that you really want to go to."

If you were going to go to some exotic destination, you wouldn't stay at the airport. You would want to explore. You would want to visit all the different places and enjoy your time there. Permissions allow us to enjoy the process. "I give myself permission to take the scenic route."

Whether you allow yourself to take the direct route or the scenic route, either way is the right way. You can learn on whichever path you take. Either path is a journey to wisdom gained from the experience.

I'm here to say that there are no permissions police. You can take anything that I've said and adjust it to make it work for you. Put your own words to it. I will say, though, that the more difficult something is to say, the more likely it is that this is an area to diligently work through. Maybe you need say it over and over until you've mastered the statement. Say it until you have come to a neutral place, as neutral as saying, "I'm wearing a blue shirt." There's no emotion in it. It's neutral, and we're totally okay with it. That's what permissions do for us.

I encourage you to say the statements out loud so you can hear yourself. "I give <u>myself</u> permission to _____." (fill in the blank). It is possible that you may need to use your name or your nickname in the statement. "I give (name) permission to _____." "I give my body permission to _____. I give my mind permission to _____." "I give myself permission to be my authentic self. It is ok to be me. It is ok to be my authentic self." "I give myself permission to take a detour in life." (To take the scenic route. To enjoy life. To receive understanding from others. To receive love from others, or to receive love from a particular person.)

The next phase in our journey together is about memories. Memory lane is sometimes enjoyable, and sometimes not. Perhaps one permission statement can be, "I give myself permission to release (a particular memory)."

Section 2

Memory Networks

Almost everyone has experienced memories or trauma that have dramatic effects across all aspects of our lives and the lives of others. What I want to look at with you here is that we are all connected to each other in many ways, but especially when it comes to our intentions, our attention, and how we focus those intentions and attention on our memories and the perspectives that relate to our emotions regarding memories and trauma and even heart rate.

We are all one. What I feel, you feel. What you feel, I feel.

In the field of quantum physics, the term <u>entanglement</u> describes a <u>universal interconnectedness</u> that is a fundamental property of all physical and biological organization. Entanglement is at the heart of the concept of the inseparability ("non-separability") of everything in the universe, even through space and time (Bradley 72).

Now, Romans 12:5 says, "For just as each of us has one body with many members, and these members do not all have the same function, so in Christ we, though many, form one body, and each member belongs to all the others"—meaning that, collectively, we form one body. While this verse refers to the body of Christ, I tend to view any group of people as though they form one body. Think for a moment about a corporation. This business is treated as a single "entity" or body. In fact, etymonline.com defines the root origin of the word "corporation" as "united in one body," from Latin corporatus (past participle of corporare) "form into a body", and corpus (genitive corporis) "body."

Whether we are talking about the body of Christ, or a business, or a family, I tend to think of any group of people as a single body. To me, they are a single unit—a team. They are individuals, yet inseparable. All we have to do is stub our little toe to know that there is no separation, and that the little toe is part of a bigger body. We don't need to think about it. The rest of the body knows instantly because the little toe "screams out" in pain. There is no distance; the reaction is instantaneous. It is the same when speaking of groups of people forming one body. Spiritually and energetically speaking, there's no distance in the body. There is no distance in the Spirit. This is a key phrase I will repeat throughout the book:

There is no distance in the Spirit.

After the crucifixion, Jesus' followers gathered together in an upper room and "with **one mind**, all of them kept devoting themselves to prayer" (Acts 1:14 NASB). Paul admonishes us to "strive for full restoration, encourage one another, be of **one mind**, live in peace. And the God of love and peace will be with you" (2 Corinthians 13:11 NIV). Paul again tells us, "Therefore if you have any encouragement from **being united** with Christ, if any comfort from his love, if any **common sharing** in the Spirit, if any tenderness and compassion, then make my joy complete by being **like-minded**, having the same love, **being one in spirit and of one mind**" (Philippians 2:1-2 NIV).

We feel others' emotions, and others can feel ours.

While interviewing Rollin McCraty, Ed Decker commented that he felt a wave of anxiety at the same moment that his mother was having a stroke 2500 miles away (Decker). With this in mind, let me point out that HeartMath Institute researchers discovered that the more connected we are in our emotions, the more passionate that we are, and the more we focus with intention, the more connected we can be to others, as though we are connected by radio waves (Bradley 87). This was the reason Mr. Decker felt his mother's anxiety even though she was so far away.

We are interconnected via our emotions.

The nervous system acts like an antenna that is tuned to and responds to the magnetic fields produced by the hearts of others. It's even possible for magnetic signals radiated by the heart of one individual to influence the brain rhythms of another (McCraty 2003 pp. 9, 11).

Think about it: We are so intricately connected, yet we are usually not aware of that interconnection and how one person's feelings and emotions have the ability to impact another person's feelings and emotions. Certainly, this can happen if we are in the same room, but it can also happen at a distance of thousands of miles if we have an emotional connection to that person.

"When people are engaged in a deep conversation, they begin to fall into a dance. They synchronize their movements, their postures, their vocal pitches, their speaking rates, even the length of pauses between respirations. What they discovered is that even their physiology can be linked and entrained" (McCraty 2003 p. 7). That's very important for us to take a look at. People are intricately connected to each other just by being in deep conversation. I'm going to extend that a bit, so bear with me. Whether we are in a conversation with someone in person, on the phone, or in our minds, we are connecting to that person and affecting ourselves, as well as the person on whom we have focused our attention.

Psalm 19:14 says, "May the words of my mouth and the meditations of my heart be pleasing in your sight." Somewhere else I read or interpreted it, "May my spoken words and my unspoken thoughts be pleasing in your sight, be acceptable." There is strong evidence that points to our thoughts being known by cells, organisms, plants, animals, and brain cells in other people (Stone 15). My point is this: When we have these conversations in our heads, we are connected to that person. We are having that conversation whether in person or in our minds. Spirit to spirit—our spirits to the other person's spirit—they can hear us.

Therefore, we want to have conversations that are going to bring harmony to our relationships. The more that we indulge in negativity, whether in thought or in words, the more others begin to feel it. Let me rephrase: If we are engaged in a negative conversation with others, in our minds or out loud, then the way that they respond to us begins to change, the way we respond to them begins to change, and we begin this dance that's not a great dance. We begin this dance that is very disruptive to our systems and our health.

Conversely, let's say we engage in a conversation with a positive attitude—even though it may be not a pleasant topic. By shifting our attitude to one of reconciliation or resolution, the conversation can have a dramatically different outcome. Think about it: If we adopt these positive attitudes, then the way we approach the conversation is different, the way the other person responds to us is different, and the way we respond to them is different.

This is especially true when we think about our memories including traumatic memories. How often do we have a conversation with someone and then walk away from that conversation thinking, "Well, I should have said this and I should have said that," because we are upset about what the other person said or the outcome of the conversation?

When we begin to obsess over what we could have said or what we should have said, we relive those conversations in our minds. During those moments, we are connected (or reconnected) to that person. It is non-local. There is no distance in the spirit. Mathematically, science has proven that there is no distance in the spirit—that these two points in time come together and become entangled, inseparable. Thus, we become entangled with the moment, the other person, and their emotions, and we entangle them in ours (Bradley pp, 77, 91).

Since we can become entangled in memories, traumas, and emotions, we will explore some different ways to help us move through the memory healing process so that not only do we receive healing, but everyone involved in that memory can as well. HeartMath research states that evidence indicates the existence of an energetic communication system that is just below our conscious awareness. It also states that our intention can influence wound healing rates, pain, hemoglobin levels, and other physiological states. Intuition also affects changes in the way DNA is shaped and the way in which water is structured (McCraty 2004b pp. 325–326). Hence, as we receive healing, we can in turn create a space so others can receive healing as well.

Central Events

In this section, we will discuss how to identify one type of "memory network" created by a "central event" that radiates outward, as depicted in the diagram below. Central events are single events in our personal histories or the histories of our lives. It is possible for a single "central" event to impact multiple people. I think of the central event like a sun that radiates outward, showing how it has touched our own lives. In turn, it can also show how the event has touched other lives. Let me clarify just a bit. In the last example, the sun rays radiating outward show the various people directly involved. But, like the sun, it extends its reach to the people that each individual involved knows. The images in this section are available in the free Bonus Materials.

Central Event
One memory that more than one person participated in.
Each person may be affected in a different way.

While a central event can impact a family, there are some events that we hear of through news sources. These larger events such as war, acts of terror, or even the death of a beloved celebrity impact us nationally, or even globally. We may not be directly involved, but the radiating outward of the event causes a ripple effect. Case in point: Most people know where they were and what they were doing when they heard about 9/11. It is a moment they will never forget. In the moments that we each experience that one event—and because we all focus our attention on that event—we are all interconnected.

For now, let's bring it back a bit and look at an event in which we were more personally involved. Let's say that your event was something that happened at school or at work, and there were, say, two or three people involved. Perhaps a central event for you was a traumatic breakup. Or it could have been an event at work during a department meeting involving the department head and two employees. Let's suppose then that there was an argument and one person felt humiliated. Anytime any single individual goes back and revisits that memory, all three are connected. Not only that, but each person has their own perspective that they bring to this memory. That one central event has a different impact on each person's life.

Let's take it one step further to say that maybe all three decide to tell someone else about the meeting—what happened and how they felt. During the re-telling or re-enactment, the person involved is connected to the event and to the people, but now *another* person is also connected to it. By listening to the story, this new person is re-living it, and the event begins radiating out a bit farther. It's a bit like social media in that regard.

What if we take a look at a more public event, like that of the death of a celebrity? Maybe the celebrity was a famous musician or actor. From minimal to profound, each person who hears about the passing of this individual will feel the impact of the celebrity's death a little bit differently, depending on whether or not they are familiar with the celebrity's work. For people who are great fans, it may impact them extremely profoundly. However, that celebrity's family, their children, their siblings, and those who lived and worked with them are impacted to an even greater degree. My point is that each person has his/her own level of trauma and emotional involvement in the memory.

Whether it was a memory that had only three people in it or whether it is a more global event, our interactions with that event/memory and the entanglement with it can then create what I call an "interference pattern" for the others who were involved, or anyone else connected with that memory via outside conversations.

Recognizing Memory Themes and Networks

When we hear ourselves say, "I will never forget," that is one way to recognize entanglement to a memory network. This continues to connect us deeply with the trauma/event/memory, and, in effect, can prolong our entanglement with it. Additionally, when we think about the event, we can project our feelings about the memory in such a way that everyone who is also connected to that event can potentially feel our emotions (to that trauma) on some level. Deciding to never forget also allows for that memory to become embedded in our system, and allows it to rise up, seemingly out of nowhere, in such a way that we relive that memory over and over and over. Any single person reenacting the memory triggers the memories of the other people who are connected with it because we are interconnected and there is no distance in the spirit.

In several audio series on time, Arthur Burk discusses this in a similar way. He points out that not only are we interconnected to each other, but we're connected to each other via the time and the land where it happened. This is really groundbreaking work, and was probably the first that started me thinking along these lines of how connected are we via time, land, and memories (Burk, 2011; Burk, 2012).[i]

Clearing the Entanglement With Memories.

I highly recommend marking this page. We will refer to it often as we move through the rest of the sections in the book. Even though we are connected via all of our memories, and it sounds like it is this big, big thing (which it is), there is a way to balance ourselves to the memories and emotions, which is really amazingly awesome. I want to walk you through an exercise that I do with my clients to help bring neutrality and resolution to these persistent memories.

First, I want you to think about an event/memory that involves you and at least one other person. In reading through some of the examples, I am sure that several things have come to mind. Pick a memory that keeps coming to mind, especially if, no matter what you do, it is always with you. This would be a memory that you think about all the time, even when you're trying not to think about it. It just won't go away. Maybe the memory stems from an argument that you had with your spouse. Maybe it is a confrontation that you had with one of your children.

Usually this is a memory that you play like a movie, hoping for a different conversation or a different outcome. I'm going to propose, at least energetically, at least emotionally, that it can have resolution, finally allowing you to let go of it.

Now that you have chosen your memory, I want you to think about that memory and imagine that you are standing in a room with the others involved. Engage with them as though they are standing right in front of you. Now, it is always a good idea to set some healthy boundaries. Therefore, I would like for you to engage with an attitude of resolution rather than accusation. I would also like for you to acknowledge the other person's perspective. We want to be heard. They also want to be heard. Collectively, we want to know that what we say matters, even if the other person does not agree. Now that you've thought about their perspective, what is yours? What do you want them to hear? What do you need to say? Maybe a lot of time has passed since the original event. Given what you know now, would you say something different? In this moment, with all you have learned since that memory originally took place, begin to tell them what you feel you need to say.

Acknowledge your own feelings. Nowhere in the Bible does it say that we cannot have anger. It does say, "Be slow to anger" (James 1:19). It also says, "Therefore each of you must put off falsehood and speak truthfully to your neighbor, for we are all members of one body. In your anger do not sin: Do not let the sun go down while you are still angry" (Ephesians 4:25-26 NIV).

Having acknowledged your own feelings, you can also acknowledge the other person's feelings. In doing so, and accepting their feelings, you can also acknowledge if their actions were inappropriate. That's the easy part—looking at the other person's actions. However, also be willing to acknowledge if and when your actions were not appropriate either.

There's ZERO judgment here. It just is what it is. Sometimes, when we speak from the heart, we speak from our emotions. We say things that we later regret. Okay. So acknowledge it. Acknowledge it the same way we acknowledge doubt. Just acknowledge it. Then I want you to release that person. Here is how it could look.

Have a conversation with someone. You do not have to be happy with the conversation. We have already acknowledged that. You do not have to be happy with the behavior on either side. Acknowledge that. Acknowledge what you feel in this memory. Anger? Sadness? Remorse? Unworthy? Betrayed? Note what those emotions are. Continue in this until you have addressed each person involved. You can address them as a group or individually.

Here's what I do next. While in this room (in my mind), and after having a conversation for resolution as described above, I say the following:

"I choose to remove all of my energy (all I have invested in this memory and all the emotions I feel about it and all that I am) from this event. I choose to release the negative emotions of _____. I also choose to release you (to no longer be entangled via the memory) so that you can choose to do the same. I choose to bless you with love and release you. I choose to bless you with the space (this ability) to be able to release this memory as well. I choose to remove my energy from this event/memory."

I stay with this until I feel (in my mind) that all has been done to bring resolution. I may spend more time blessing them (which we will discuss further in Section 5), or on some other aspect of the conversation, until I feel it is resolved. Because of entanglement, it is possible that the other(s) involved in the memory have not been able to release themselves from the memory. That is a possibility. So my thoughts are more of a reminder to myself so that I am not hindering anyone else in their healing of memories. There is no way of knowing exactly what the impact of this memory has on each person involved. It's more to cover all the bases, so to speak.

Once you have said what you need to say to each person involved, and chosen (or given yourself permission to choose and then made the choice) to release yourself from the memory, imagine walking out of the room. All of your energy follows you out the door. Your energy can look like anything you want, as long as you can envision the energy going out the door with you.

Similar to adjoining rooms at a hotel, we discover at this point that there are actually two doors to close. First close their door to you via that memory and emotion, then close your door to them via that one memory. Think of this as "shaking the dust off your feet."

You have now removed your energy from this memory, and you have given them the space to do the same thing. You've blessed them with the ability to release it in the same way that you're releasing it.

Cleaning the Energy

The energy that came with you out of that room has lots of negative emotions in it. In the same way that we like to wear clean clothes, we like to have clean energy. What is one of the best ways to get clean? Take a shower.

Imagine a shower with a big rain head. Imagine now that the water that comes from the shower is filled with emotions that are opposite to the negative ones. Imagine love, refreshing peace, appreciation for your inherent value (and any other feel-good emotion you want to bring in) all washing over you, removing all the negativity and washing it all down the drain.

When you feel like all the negativity is gone, imagine that this rain is now washing through your body and filling you up so that there is no room for the negative. Then turn off the rain shower and imagine that, along with the negative emotions washing away, the room behind the door is now being completely destroyed and whisked away, never to come back.

Making Room for the Good

In the old room's place, bring in a room that is filled with the positive emotions you want to feel. Imagine that you now have a room where you feel love and acceptance and honor (or any of the feel-good emotions from your shower. Open the door and stand in this new room. Stand surrounded by those emotions. Bask in the healing warmth. Absorb all that there is. Stay in this room as long as you like.

When you walk out of your new room, leave the door open so that you can revisit this room filled with these emotions as often as you like. What you will find is that you are more neutral to that memory now, and the interactions of those involved in that memory with you are different.

Since you have acknowledged this person, you will find that, even if you don't talk to them a lot, that memory that was coming to your mind over and over and over is going to begin to diminish, and, in some cases, rather quickly.

Candice Pert's groundbreaking research introduced us to the concept of the biochemical nature of emotions within our bodies, and that those chemicals "form a dynamic information network, linking mind and body." The basic premise of her work, *Molecules of Emotion*, is that emotions have a physical, chemical component within our body (Pert). Releasing the emotions and memories begins a physical process of releasing these emotional chemicals from our bodies. Hence, the body will physically process this part of the healing.

What you may find, then, is that you experience some physical detoxing from this exercise because the body is now physically releasing the memory and the emotions. As it is doing this, you become more and more neutral to the event/memory. Once we are fully neutral to an event/memory, it may never come to mind again. If it does, we can acknowledge it as an event in our lives, but it no longer has the same physiological effects on our bodies as it did before.

Take a deep breath. Breathe in life. Breathe in feel-good emotions such as joy, harmony, and exuberance. Take a full deep breath in, then a full exhale out, and see how that feels. What you have just done brings healing to the whole of you as a person, physically, emotionally, mentally, and spiritually. This shifts your energy and your perspectives in such a way that everyone around you shifts theirs in response.

When I shift, others shift.

This shift in perspectives changes the way that we respond to each other. If I am more neutral to this memory, then the way that I respond to others—to the people in my life, to the people who are involved in the memory—will be different. It will shift. Moving forward, my attitude can be one of more compassion. No longer do I need to play the game of back and forth, with everyone feeling bad. I chose resolution. I chose compassion. I can now choose to feel good. I give myself permission to release this. I give myself permission to feel good emotions.

Memory Themes

Memory Themes
Many memories that all seem to be part of a common theme.

Similar to the diagram for central events, memory themes have a central thought, central emotion, and/or central belief that is built from many similar memories and/or emotions. The theme radiates outward and is balanced in the same way as central events. In order to move forward in the healing of memory themes, we should determine what could be included in any given theme. I want to note that, as we move through these examples, we will do the same steps as the central event exercise. But because the focus is slightly different, we will call this one the "Central Theme Exercise" to help us distinguish our focus, our intentions, and our attentions.

Central Theme of a Relationship Breakup

When I hear a client telling me that they have experienced a serious relationship breakup (such as divorce or death of a spouse), I often observe various themes coming to my mind. One sub-theme may be the relationship timeline: from meeting the person to the "beginning of the end" all the way through to the end. Emotional sub-themes may all center around anger, frustration, jealousy, betrayal, abandonment, loss, grief, and perhaps even hatred or animosity. There may be other sub-themes, as well as a few central events interspersed within this theme. The central events may need to be dealt separately before doing the exercise on the central theme.

Doing the central theme exercise with this or a similar theme in mind, you can address it in as many sections or pieces as you like. The more you practice with the technique, the more you will be able to "bundle" into the room. Feel free to spend time now working through the themes that have come to mind—or you may choose to finish Section 2 and do it then.

Central Theme of Long-Term Illness (of You or a Loved One)

When I hear a client tell me that they are battling a long-term illness such as cancer, I observe many, many themes. For this type of theme, I ask questions such as: What led up to the illness? Do we know the causative factor of the illness? What memories surround hearing the diagnosis? Who was involved along the way? Doctors, nurses, lab technicians, other clinicians, family, friends? What about the physical roads traveled to and from appointments and treatments? What about the roads traveled in the mind (fears, disappointment, grief, etc.)? Where did all this take place—the locations of these events? Doctors' offices, hospital treatment rooms, hospital waiting rooms, labs, clinics, etc.?

This theme is a very big one to work with. You may want to break it down into several exercises so that it is more manageable. Follow the questions above and do the exercise for each question, while keeping in mind how you feel so that when you bring in the positive emotions, you know what you are washing away. Continue to do the exercise for each set of questions until you feel that you have completed it to the best of your ability. We will cover more aspects when we move through later sections in the book.

Emotional Themes

Emotional Theme
One emotion that may have several variations such as:
Anger: frustration, irritation, mad
Grief: sorrow, loss, pain

With emotional themes, we may not know why we feel a particular emotion, but still feel as though it is an ever-present part of us. It is possible that we may have inherited a pre-disposition to that emotion, or that we naturally fell into it sometime in our lives. Either way, this emotion, either by inheritance or out of a habit of entertaining it, has become a "go-to" emotion. There may be a variety of memories that all are tagged with this emotion. By addressing the emotion as a theme, we can begin to release memories associated with it quicker and more easily.

As an example, if we feel as though we can never state our opinions, or that we are not important enough for others to listen to us, then the theme could be feeling "belittled," "shut down," "unimportant," or "ignored." Other emotional themes can be belittlement, fear, the need for perfection, the fear of rejection, or the fear of not being accepted. However, if the go-to emotion is anger, then we look at the anger as being a response to something else. It is likely that the theme is not the anger, but that the anger is ignited by the actual theme.

In working through the steps of the central theme exercise, we may be addressing many memories and/or whole groups of people collectively. As you stand in this room that holds all of the memories, emotions, people, and locations involved, you can address them individually or you can address them as a group.

If, while you address them as a group, there is an individual person, place, or emotion comes to mind, then work through that one individually. Keep going through the steps of addressing what is in the room until you feel you have done all you can. Then move on to the other steps to complete this process.

Memory Networks

In this section, we will determine how to identify the second type of "memory network" that is created by others' memories, and how those people approach us throughout our interactions in life. The images in this section are available in the free Bonus Materials.

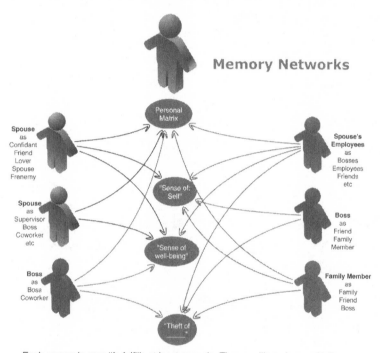

Each person in your life fulfills at least one role. They are like spheres of influence that rotate around you and impact various areas of your life. A single person play the roles of confidant, friend, lover, spouse. In family businesses, that same person may also be your boss or supervisor.

Each person's wounds will have a unique impact on how they fulfill that role and how they interact with you.

There may be more than one theme of memories, belief systems, or fears/phobias that needs to be highlighted in order to balance the effect they have on your life.

The center circles represent how these people impact your life. There may be one or many circles. These are just examples of what each one could be.

As depicted by the diagram above, it is likely and highly probable for a person in your life to have central events that radiate out to you and affect you in very specific ways. In fact, there may be multiple central events or memory themes involved.

Depending on the relationships we have with certain people, we may find that they play multiple roles in our lives. Our grandmother may also be our teacher or mentor. A memory as grandmother may have a different impact on us than when we view her as a mentor.

Similarly, our spouses can have many roles in our lives, such as spouse, protector, nurturer, friend, lover, coworker, or boss. Therefore, it is not only possible, but very likely that there is an entire network of memories and themes regarding these people in our lives and how they affect us. This is especially true when the relationship crosses the boundary lines between professional/business life and personal life.

Since it is often difficult for people to separate business from personal feelings, one person may express outrage over work conditions, but it feels as though this person delivered a personal insult. Perhaps we feel belittled. Perhaps we feel the other person has unrealistic expectations of us, or that they expect us to be perfect in our jobs. At home or away from work, there may be different sets of memories, each with its own set of themes.

How can these memory themes and networks impact your life? Let's say that we grew up with a friend who then becomes our coworker and later becomes our supervisor. Depending on how various situations are handled with our "supervisor," we may determine that our very personhood feels the impact due to personal insults. Or we may find that our overall energy or vitality has been drained.

In extreme cases, we may feel as though our individuality, our personhood, or our autonomy has been stolen or lost. Perhaps we feel as though our sense of self, our confidence, or even our dignity has been diminished. How confident and capable we feel may be impacted because of these memory themes. As we move through the exercise, make note of the theme and how it has impacted all the various areas of life.

I'll emphasize again that it is important to have healthy boundaries. We do not want to walk in victimhood. We want to walk in victory. As Arthur Burk said, "The best way to not be a victim is to have really good boundaries." So I will side-step just a bit, because invariably someone will ask how to deal with people who tend to make things personal.

Here are words you can use: "I can see that you may be having a very bad day, but don't make it personal." "I understand that you have this task that you need done. Let's see what we can do to resolve it." "How may I best support you?" By making these statements and asking how we can best support them, we are neutralizing the situation and helping bring some measure of clarity to ourselves, as well as the others involved. Note that I did not say "help." I said "support."

Generally, when we ask someone, "Gee, are you having a bad day?" they will often take a deep breath and respond with something like, "Well, okay, I know it's not about you, but I'm just so frustrated." By approaching them in this manner, we are not judging. We are not resonating with their frustrations. A non-judgmental attitude keeps us from approaching each other through our woundedness of "Are we good enough?" or "Am I capable?" or other doubts that plague us. We are then better able to release the trauma—not playing the game of throwing darts at each other, but actually being able to find some resolution.

We will follow the same steps as we did in the central event and central theme exercises, this time identifying the memory networks of any number of interconnected events and themes, and how they impact your life. Remember that, rather than with an accusatory attitude, we approach the conversation with an attitude of reconciliation or resolution.

Words like "You always" or "You never"—"You always belittle me," "You never pay attention to me,"—may give you a clue as to the theme. Don't look at accusation. Look at the theme. What is the theme? Remember to attempt to view the situation from all perspectives, including theirs. We are using our imagination to have this conversation. In doing so, we are connected to them. Even if we have this conversation in our minds, we are connecting to them and they are hearing us on some level.

What you may discover is that they approached the event with a wounded spirit. They may feel that things need to be perfect, because if they as a person are not perfect, they might not receive love. People often act from a fear of being rejected. This may be their woundedness.

Recognizing and acknowledging the wound and then releasing ourselves and others from this memory—releasing ourselves and others from this theme—and making a choice (giving ourselves permission to do something different, to receive praise instead of belittlement, to receive the good instead of the bad, to receive acceptance instead of rejection) can begin to shift and clear the network.

The fact that we address the memories and themes for ourselves clears enough in us that the others may naturally find resolution for themselves as well. Because the emotions and the energy is released from you, it is also released from the situation and all others involved. In this manner the others involved are no longer bound to that negativity unless they choose to be; therefore, healing can come to everyone.

Like the central theme exercise, working through this network may take a little more diligence because there may be many themes involved. The good thing is that, by knowing the technique, we can do the exercise as many times as necessary until all the events and themes have been addressed. So if we forget some aspect or another, we can do the exercise for that when it comes to our minds.

Positive Connections

In the same way that we can be connected via the negative, we are also connected via the positive. We can experience joy in our memories. When our memory is a fun memory, it is a good memory for us and brings positive emotions and healing. In thinking about these relationship networks, it is good to remember why we were attracted to this person in the first place—whether it's as a friend, a lover, a spouse, or whatever role that person plays in our lives, there are always good memories to be able to think on.

Having replaced the old room with a new one, bring that joy or positive emotion into your new room and bask in its warmth, like being cocooned in a warm blanket. Begin that feel-good process. Focus attention on positive memories. Looking at the same person involved in the memory networks, what is the positive memory? Think on that positive memory you have. Can you engage in that memory with an attitude of appreciation because you have learned something great and valuable, something that helps you to truly appreciate the roles that they play in your life? Bask in that appreciation; bask in that acceptance; bring that energy in and see how it feels.

Notes

Section 3

The God Session

The purpose of doing any personal growth work is to heal our woundedness, to gain wisdom, and to move through life with more ease, peace, and tranquility. While life is not always smooth, as long as we are willing to learn from the trials that come our way, we can gain wisdom from the experience. Life's pitfalls become easier to navigate and we are less likely to have that same scenario come our way again and again.

Non-Judgment

The thought process of non-judgment is one concept I learned early on when I first started working with the BodyTalk System. The adage of "If you spot it, you got it" is indeed true. In fact, the Biblical analogy of the splinter and log demonstrates this very principle. There are some situations that we respond to with neutrality, and there are others to which we overreact. In the moment of that overreaction, we can choose to look at how connected or entangled we are with the situation and what is happening around us. Sometimes it's easier for us to see our stuff in other people than it is to see it in us. While I cannot confirm this, I have heard it said that Dr. Phil's dad uses the phrase, "My stuff doesn't look very good on that person." I like the picture I get when I hear that phrase, as it sums up our overreactions very succinctly.

Matthew 7:1–4 (NIV) says, "Do not judge, or you too will be judged. For in the same way you judge others, you will be judged, and with the measure you use, it will be measured to you. Why do you look at the speck of sawdust in your brother's eye and pay no attention to the plank in your own eye? How can you say to your brother, 'Let me take the speck out of your eye,' when all the time there is a plank in your own eye?"

John 7:24 (NIV) says, "Stop judging by mere appearances, but instead judge correctly."

John 7:24 (NLT): "Look beneath the surface so you can judge correctly."

Non-judgment is a very important concept for us to explore. We judge out of our woundedness.

We set our standards, and we must live up to them. When we see someone else not adhering to our own impossible standards, it triggers our fears of never measuring up or being perfect enough. Thus, judgment comes out of our own fears. As though it is a coat that we put on, when we judge we step into that judgment and those fears. Energetically, we are actually putting ourselves into that person's shoes or energy field, and we can actually create a big interference for them and a big hindrance to our own healing. And the reverse is true when the other person does the same towards us.

We Are All Connected

Remember that when we are in conversation with someone—especially if it is a passionate discussion—we begin a subtle dance, and our physiology can become linked and entrained (McCraty 2003 p. 7). Not only that, but we begin resonating with their wounds because our wounds are similar. Kishori Aird stated this nicely when she said, "Any danger or threat we experience as a child holds us in its grip because the wound is electromagnetic and continues to respond to our experiences. It continuously seeks out other frequencies in resonance with its own . . . . When we have an argument with someone, especially a partner, when one of the partners falls back into childhood, they begin to emit vibrational pulses, setting up a ripple effect reaction in the brain of the spouse who is in resonance" (Aird 42).

Therefore, in whatever manner we approach a conversation with someone, we begin to resonate with each other based on our attitudes. Thus, if we approach a conversation with an attitude of reconciliation and resolution, we are more quickly able to attain that resolution without creating memory networks.

It is possible to approach a situation without judgment or to be willing to at least recognize that we may be experiencing the emotion of judgment. If we acknowledge the feelings of judgment, then it is easier to look at our own areas of personal growth.[ii]

The Splinter and the Log

My view of the splinter (speck) and the log in the Bible is this: If we see some behavior in our neighbor (the splinter in their eye), and if <u>that</u> splinter or speck is similar to our behavior, then the speck and the wood come from the same source. We see it and recognize it in others because it is the same kind of behavior that we have. But logs are bigger than splinters, which is why we work on our part rather than working on the splinter that belongs to another. It is God's way of showing us our own stuff when we encounter it in our daily lives. When we continue to see this behavior in others, we are trying to find a balance. We are trying to find a way to heal those wounds. We are trying to find a resolution.

When my children were little, I would get exasperated and exclaim, "God, they just are not listening." "Yes," He replied, "I understand." "I wish they would obey!" I cried. "Oh, yes. I definitely understand that one," He said with a smile. In that simple exchange, He showed me that He (as the parent) and me (as His child) were having the same issue. That what I complained of wasn't about my children. It was about me. Was I listening? No. Was I obedient? No. After that, I adopted the phrase, "All you need to do is look at your children to understand what God is trying to teach you." Since then, my children have grown, and I have expanded that to say that all I need to do is look at the others around me and how I react to them to know what God is trying to teach me.

Honest Assessment and Right Judgment

When we look at our own stuff and are able to address it honestly and forthrightly, then the degree of agitation and overreaction diminishes greatly. In my definition of judging rightly, I am willing to take that honest look at my part, at my stuff, and deal with it. I do so without judging myself. Then there is no need to judge another person. I can accept that others have their own processes.

Have you ever faced the same situations over and over again? Maybe with different people, but similar in the situations? I hear clients ask, "Why do all my co-workers do this?" or "Why have all my bosses treated me this way?" How many people get married, divorced, and remarried more than once, only to have the same issues with each spouse? It is almost as though all of the spouses were the same person; they just had different faces and different names.

A businessman's wife came to see me, upset because her husband had lost his job. Many years ago, they'd had a similar predicament in which he had lost his job. They had bills to pay, mouths to feed, and responsibilities to fulfill. She admitted that the first time this happened she told God, "I don't care what the lesson is. He just needs a job!" Miraculously, he found a job the very next day. But by not being willing to learn the lesson, they found themselves in the same situation not twice, but three times. When she came to see me, my question to her was, "Are you willing to look at what lessons are to be learned?"

Maybe you have experienced something similar. Perhaps the question is one of permissions: I give myself permission to learn my life lessons. I don't have to like them. I just need to be able to get through them.

When we look at the memory network exercises that we did in Section 2, let's ask, "Am I willing to look at my part in the memory? Am I willing to take responsibility for my actions in the memory and be able to address it in a non-judgmental way?"

Setting a Platform for Success

I know this to be true: We continue to learn life lessons until the day that we transition from this life. The women in my family are long-lived, which means that I have a lot of learning still ahead of me. Philippians 1:6 says, "Being confident of this, that he who began a good work in you will carry it on to completion until the day of Christ Jesus." My life lessons won't be complete until the day I transition, and that looks to be a long time away. And yet, while I'm not a completed work yet, while my lessons are not yet done, I can give myself permission to view myself in a non-judgmental way. I know that I can have compassion and appreciation for the work that I have done so far, and for the work I am going to be doing. I can view those opportunities as growth opportunities while accepting myself without judgment.

I also know this to be true: Our children and grandchildren observe the manner in which we live our lives, and they will likely mirror some of those same characteristics. If we are willing to learn the lessons that come our way, then their observations are positive and fruitful. We can pass along the wisdom that we gain and place a platform under our children and grandchildren for their success. If, however, we are unwilling to learn those lessons, then by those same observations they may inherit our patterns and predispositions, leading them to make the same mistakes or to learn lessons that were intended for a previous generation.

My preference is that we give our children and future descendants the platform needed to walk in victory. They will have their own paths to walk, their own lessons to learn, their own wisdom to gain—they need not add ours.

With this attitude of non-judgment in mind, let's revisit permissions and memory networks. Let's look at the exercise again, especially if the memory was difficult to work through. One way to gain perspective is to look at the event as though it were a movie. Another way is to look at it as though it had happened to somebody else besides us. What advice would we give to someone else? What would we tell that person? That advice is what we are telling ourselves.

Sometimes it is easier to feel compassion for a stranger. Once we look at another's perspective, it is easier to remember that we are all human, that no one is perfect. At that point, we can begin to feel compassion for the woundedness. We release our own wounds and release our connectedness to the woundedness of the other people. Our ability to look at the situation with a little bit of distance allows us some compassion, which helps others to release their woundedness as well. Then we can come into a place of respect and have the ability to release and resolve those wounds and the negative emotions that are in those wounds/memories, and in doing so embrace the positive emotions, including the appreciation that we feel not only for ourselves, but also for other people.

Redefine Failure. Redefine Success.

I'd like to redefine the word failure. Failure is missing the mark. I've heard the same thing said about sin: Sin is missing the mark. Judgment would say that the failure is a bad thing, but in reality, it is through our mistakes that we learn and grow.

Instead, let's focus our attention on what life might look like without the pain of woundedness, guilt, shame, and judgment. Let's focus on what life would be like with wisdom, acceptance of self, and peace. What does it feel like? What does it look like? What is that picture?

Now let's think about what it means to move in a different direction. Moving in a different direction is one definition of repentance. When we repent, we move in a different direction. We move in the opposite direction, and in the opposite spirit. Matthew 3:8 (NLT) says, "Produce fruit in keeping with repentance." However, Weymouth New Testament translates this verse as, "Therefore let your lives *prove* your change of heart."

Archers and Their Targets

Think of archers who spot their targets, set their stances, notch their arrows, then raise the bows, aim, and shoot. They might hit their targets; they might not. They might hit the bull's eye; they might not. But if they miss the <u>*intended target*</u>, they shift everything so that they are now moving in a different direction, however slight it may be. They practice and they practice and they practice until they can hit the target. They know where they want the arrow to fly, and they will not stray from that (to the best of their ability). There is no room for judgment and beating themselves up. There is only honest assessment.

Let us look at where we want to go—our path in life, our end destination. That is permissions without judgment. I give myself permission to assess my intended destination. I give myself permission to do the best I know how, given the time, resources, and information that I have in the moment. I give myself permission to shift so that I can attain my intended goal. I give myself permission to move in a new direction.

Golf

My husband loves golf, so it is never a surprise to see golf on TV at our house. During a particular pro-am tournament (and I can't remember which one because I'm not the golf person in the family), I happened to catch a moment when Nick Faldo was coaching an amateur. It was one of those five-minute coaching lessons in the middle of the pro-am.

Since it has been a few years, I will retell to the best of my recollection: Nick Faldo and an amateur were on screen setting up the lesson for the viewing audience. Nick says to the amateur, "What do you want to work on today?" The amateur responds, "I don't want to slice." Nick Faldo said to the man matter-of-factly, "And you see, that's the problem." The amateur said, "I don't understand." Sir Nick said, "When you say, 'Whatever happens, I don't want to slice,' then you immediately give your subconscious mind a picture of slicing the ball, and off it goes in the wrong direction. Your subconscious mind sees that picture and says, 'Oh, that's what you want me to do.' And because of the imagery you have given, the subconscious says, 'Got it. I'll make it happen.'" Sir Nick continued, "When you take your stance and hit the ball, the body follows that picture that you just gave your subconscious mind."

"If you want to hit the green, if you want to make it there in the shortest way possible, then," he said, "the best thing to do is look at the green. Look at where you want to go. Look at the straightest way for that ball to get to the green. See the ball going that way. It's a little bit of visual imagery. See the ball, see the green. Give the correct picture to your subconscious mind. When you line up to hit that ball, you're going to be much straighter than you would have been otherwise because of your subconscious mind. Your body has that in mind."

How do we move forward with that? We need to find the picture where we want to be. Find the words that match that picture. By doing so, we are much more likely to hit our targets, to get to that green, to be on the right path because our subconscious minds have images to work with.

Clean, Fresh Air

When I was a child of about seven or eight years, I knew lots of people who smoked. I would say, "Why do you smoke? Why do you smoke?" Finally, a family member said, "I'm going to quit smoking." Later he came back and said, "I'm not going to quit smoking." I was so upset. Then he said, "I don't want to be a quitter. I choose to breathe clean, fresh air." He painted a picture with words that made it easier to move in a different direction. This always stuck with me.

Isn't it interesting that we don't associate quitting with positivity? So instead of "quitting" (because we don't want to be quitters), choose to breathe clean, fresh air. I make a conscious choice to breathe clean, fresh air.

Some would say, "I am going to begin not smoking," because it is a beginning of something new. But again, what picture does this give? Usually the associated imagery is an empty ashtray with cigarettes. Not a pleasant picture. It leaves the person feeling agitated. By saying, "I choose to breathe clean, fresh air," the body naturally gravitates away from smoke and cigarettes. These words bring to mind a more pleasant image, and the body responds naturally.

"I choose to breathe clean, fresh air." "I give myself permission to breathe clean, fresh air." "I choose to hit the target." "I choose to be on course." There might be a few variations or deviations, and we might sometimes miss the mark. But when we know what we want and we have that picture in mind, it's easier to achieve the intended goal.

The God Session: Quickest Answered Prayers

I find the quickest way to get prayers answered is what I call a "God session." In a God session, I say, "Gee, I'm not really sure how to approach this. I'm going to let you take care of this, God." Sometimes it is easier said than done, and sometimes it's very, very easy. The more that you do it, the easier it gets.

It looks something like this in the beginning: Sometimes I know what it is that I want or need. I might not have the words, but I'm willing to look at my stuff. I'm willing to look at what my life lessons are, and gain that wisdom. I'm willing to move in that new direction.

Frank Conversations

I am also willing to have a very frank conversation, saying something such as, "I don't like this. I don't like the road I'm on. It ended. It came to an abrupt halt in the middle of a raging river, and there's no bridge, and I know I need to be on the other side. I'm not very happy about going into that cold water. I might get swept away. I don't really want to do that. I need you to send me a lifeline here. I'd like for you to pick me up and move me to the other side. I'd settle for a bridge. At the very least, I need you to send me a rope that I can hold on to."

By approaching the conversation with frank honesty and a willingness to look at my own stuff, I can say what I think. I might even have a temper tantrum. God, in renewing His mercies every day (Lamentations 3:22–23), may not like my temper tantrums, but He forgives me (1 John 1:9). Not only that, but it gives us (God and me) a starting place much closer to the end goal because we don't have to backtrack to look at my issues. Being willing to start any conversation with honesty and integrity saves time, and it certainly helps me get through the tough parts more quickly.

Nobody says we have to like the process. Nobody says we have to enjoy it. Obviously it is easier if we *can* like and enjoy the process, but there is absolutely no judgment just because we don't like it.

I might not like walking through the river, but I know that the best thing that will ever happen to me is getting to the other side, looking back at the experience, and saying, "No, I don't want to have to do that again, but man, I learned so much. It's the best thing that ever happened to me." Honest assessment and acknowledgement definitely help. In the meantime, I am perfectly willing to say, "I don't like this. I don't want to do this." At least I'm honest about it.

"I believe, Lord. Help my unbelief. I don't want to do that." There is my resistance. I will recognize it, I will give voice to it, but then I will start to move in the direction that I know is the right path for me to take and the right lesson to learn. "I give myself permission to learn and grow, even if I don't know how, and even if I don't like it.

Hebrews 4:16 says. "Let us then approach God's throne of grace with confidence, so that we may receive mercy and find grace to help us in our time of need." I acknowledge that I don't like it. I acknowledge there's a bigger picture. I acknowledge that I plan to move in that direction, to move through that lesson, and therefore I can come boldly to the throne. I can come to the throne with confidence and be able to say, very frankly, how I feel and what I want.

Psalm 55:22 (NCV) states, "Give your worries to the Lord, and he will take care of you."

1 Peter 5:7 (NCV) says, "Give all your worries to him, because he cares about you."

Philippians 4:6–7 says, "Be anxious for nothing, but in everything by prayer and supplication, *with thanksgiving*, let your request be made known to God." Acknowledge what your emotions are and where your doubts are, but with thankfulness and gratitude, know there's a bigger picture. It goes on, "And the peace of God, which surpasses all comprehension, will guard your hearts and minds in Christ Jesus."

The God Session: Wonder and Awe

The next part of this God session would look something like this: "Gee, I wonder what that means? Gee, I wonder how that works?" I have this kind of conversation all the time. I'm curious and I start a conversation. "Wouldn't it be nice? Wouldn't it be nice to not have to go across that river? Wouldn't it be nice to be able to bring the other side of the river to me? Wouldn't that be nice?" I am not really sure how that would happen, but I can always ask, and in the asking, I can release it to God.

I have these questions about how things happen. When it comes to faith, there are some things that we just know are true. We know it deep in our gut. We know it in our knower. The small intestine is what we sometimes call our "knower." "I know it in my knower." My classic illustration is the fast answer in the story of the luggage.

Luggage and the Request

We were living in California and flying back home for a visit. The secretary where we attended church said that she was always "tied to her luggage" when she traveled. She always prayed that she was tied to her luggage. Because of this, she never lost her luggage. I thought, "That's a fabulous idea. I'm going to do that." And so I did. But I was very curious about <u>how</u> it worked. I had no question that it did work. I just really wanted to know how.

Now to set this up for you: We had two toddlers, and everything that comes with the travel needs of two small children. In addition, we had quite a bit of luggage on the return trip. My husband is a hunter, and fills our freezer with good, organic meat to last us through the year. On our return trip, we had several meat coolers as part of our luggage. I wanted to make sure that the meat made it all the way home. It had been frozen, but we had several hours of travel and I didn't want it to thaw out or get lost. I prayed that we were tied to our luggage. It never dawned on me that I wouldn't be tied to my luggage. There was no doubt for me in that assertion. However, we were delayed because of storms. Coming into Dallas/Fort Worth, we were quite late. In fact, we landed five minutes before the next plane was supposed to take off.

The airport actually provided a golf cart to help us get from farthest end of one terminal to the farthest end of the other terminal. The golf cart was waiting for us as we got off the plane. There was no doubt in my mind that we were tied to our luggage, but I was still trying to figure out how this works. I asked the golf cart driver, "What about our luggage?" He said, "It's a straight shot for the luggage. The luggage carts don't have to drive around the curves. They can drive from one plane to the next. If you make it, your luggage will make it." I just sat back and thought, "That's actually rather brilliant, God. And that is amazingly cool."

As we got to the gate, the gate attendant asked us to hurry on down the jetway. She said they had not closed the doors yet. As we walked down that corridor, I looked out the window and saw the coolers and luggage going up the ramp and into the cargo hold of plane. I thought, "That is the most awesome thing in the whole wide world." I was thoroughly enthralled with how this worked. As we get to the door of the plane though, the attendant said, "No, you can't get on the plane." I said, "But our luggage is on the plane. I just saw it go up the ramp." She said, "You will have to take the next plane. Your luggage will be waiting for you." Then she said, "We'll give you $200 per person for the next flight." I thought, "That's pretty cool."

As we headed back to the gate attendant, I was thinking, "I'm still tied to my luggage. Okay, God, how does this work then? Are you going to put angels over it? Are you going to put a supernatural cooling agent over it so the meat doesn't spoil? How does this work exactly?"

When I reach the gate attendant, I said, "They told us that the plane was full and we couldn't get on, and that you were going to give us $200 a person to wait for the next flight." She said, "We're not doing that today." She was rather emphatic about it. I said, "Well, but that's what she told us." She repeated, "We're not doing that today," and promptly picked up the phone to call the attendant on the plane. She said, "We're not giving vouchers today. No, we are not doing that today." The next thing I heard her say was, "I don't care. Make them get off." When she hung up the phone, she said, "You need to go back down to the plane. They will let you on now."

To my utter amazement, the airline made four standby passengers get off the plane and wait for the next flight. Since all the seats were filled, as they put us on the plane they had to rearrange seats with other passengers so that I could sit with our children. They seated my husband somewhere else in the plane, not too far away.

Now I was really in wonder because we really were tied to our luggage. Even though I had no doubt in my mind that it was true, I still wondered how it worked. In a very demonstrable way, God showed me exactly how it worked. It is wonder and awe and awesomeness to be able to watch that play out.

My request still would have been honored had I gone with a rote prayer. I wouldn't have been able to witness the inner workings of the process. It started with a conversation: "How does that work?" It's often one of my conversations, as I see something, to say, "I don't really understand that. What does that mean?" Then it will come to me.

Most of these kinds of prayers are answered very, very quickly for me. In fact, they are answered within a matter of days or weeks. I admit there have been a handful of them that unfolded over time, but there is a natural conversation and willingness to understand that there is something bigger that God wants to unfold for me, if only I am willing to have the conversation and let that happen.

What is interesting is that when I got ready to write this book, I knew that what I was present to you was true, and that it was needed, and that I was supposed to write it. But I kept saying, "It sure would be nice to have resources that back up what I know to be true. I'm sure it's out there, I just don't know where to find it." Even in saying that, I had not truly released it.

"God does not always pay on Friday, but He always pays on time." (unknown)

What happened then is that a few days before I was planning to actually sit down to write the book—concepts and outline in hand, ready to write—I had a massive amount of research that I stumbled across. It literally was as though it had been dumped into my lap. My request was answered and I received the research I knew was out there. Then I realized that I had received it after I was willing to let go and proceed without it. I didn't want to write without it. That was a raging river I did not want to cross.

The interesting thing about asking the curiosity questions is that in asking the question, it is easy to let it go. It's almost more of a musing. The quicker you can let it go, the quicker the answer comes to you. That's what happened with the luggage. But with the missing research, I was trying to make it happen with my own effort, and I still couldn't find what I needed. The moment that I made the determination that I was willing to cross the raging river of writing the book, I gave myself permission and became willing to move forward to cross the river. Then all the research landed in my lap. Hence, it was a lot easier to get to the other side because I now had the bridge. I had what I needed in order to pull everything together into a cohesive whole. Once I let go of it, there it was.

Daily Conversations

One of the best ways to get prayers answered very, very quickly is to make a bold request and start a conversation. The more conversations we have, the easier it is to move through the day in continual conversation. 1 Thessalonians 5:17 says, "Pray without ceasing" or "Pray continually." What I described above is just one conversation. I have many conversations as I go through my day.

Make Thy Requests. Be Thou Not Tied to the Outcome.

By making a request but not being tied to the outcome and not needing to control the outcome, we get answers more quickly. Having said that, sometimes we have to give ourselves permission to go boldly to the throne. Perhaps we have been told that God judges us. However, He does not judge doubt. He does say, "Come believing." But when we acknowledge that we have doubts, when we acknowledge that we're not sure how things are supposed to be, He honors that and shows us.

What does this look like in an actual conversation? Either out loud or in my head I will say, "You know what, God? I need to make a request. I need the research for this book." Then I say, "Today, right now, that's my request. You may have something better in mind, and I'm okay with that, but I feel like I need to make this request for me, for my own peace of mind."

At that point I might talk a little bit more about it. I might say what kind of research I was really wishing that I could get. That I'm willing to move forward without it, but man, if I could just have that research, it sure would be nice. Here is my request. This is what I need. This is what I want, and I'm only making this request because it's for my own peace of mind. I'll acknowledge that. I know you might have something better, but this is what I want. This is my request.

I might continue saying that over and over, because I might be needing to convince myself that I'm okay with a different outcome. I keep going through this process until I have peace and a knowledge that I've been heard, and that I can actually let go of the outcome. In fact, I sometimes later forget that I even made the request. When I get the answer, a still small voice says, "Well, you did ask." Yup, I sure did.

For many people, making the request is only half the battle. Sometimes we must give ourselves permission to make the request. Sometimes we need to have permission to go boldly to the throne. Sometimes we need to have permission to make the request boldly. At some point, we need to give ourselves permission to actually receive answer.

Let's revisit our memory network exercises. Do you have a room that is filled with an emotion such as fear? Fear of not being heard. Fear of not being acknowledged. Fear of not getting your prayer answered. Maybe the emotion in your room is disappointment or anger, or maybe it's depression. Whatever it is, as we've been talking about the God session, look at that emotion and go to that room, and then walk out of that room and bring all of your energy with you, closing the door behind you.

Imagine that room behind the door being completely destroyed and whisked away, never to come back. Then, in its place, bring in a room that is filled with the positive emotions you want to feel. Build a room that is the opposite of fear. Our next section explores the opposite of fear. We want to build the room so that you have the space to hold the positive emotions and energy that are the opposite of fear. Walk into a room full of potential and possibilities. A room where God can do anything. A room where you can receive your own personal miracle.

Notes

Section 4

Heart Code

Opposites of Fear

What is the opposite of fear? There are four, in fact. The first one is truth, the second is trust, the third is clarity, and the fourth is love. Remember we talked about moving in a different direction? Moving in a different direction to the opposite of fear would be to move or walk with truth, trust, clarity, and love. On my path, I learned of trust first, but later reordered these four as: Truth, Trust, Clarity, and Love.

When we know the truth—not my version of the truth, not your version of the truth, but the Absolute Truth—then we begin to be able to trust that truth. We can trust what we <u>know</u> to be true. When we can trust that, it gives us more clarity. Having more clarity makes it easier to accept or give love. Before we discuss the others, I would like to introduce a definition of love that is different than what most people have.

Redefine Love

Driving home one day, I heard this verse in my head: "Love God, love your neighbor as you love yourself. Love your neighbor in exactly the same manner as you love yourself." I remember thinking, "What does that mean?" (There is my God session.) "I don't understand. I need a little more clarity. What does that mean?"

Love your neighbor as you love yourself (Leviticus 19:18).

What does it mean to love someone <u>as</u> you love yourself? It means <u>in the same manner</u> as you love yourself. Most people hear "Love God," and answer, "Uh huh, and love others." BUT the scripture actually translates, "Love God, love your neighbor (love another person) in the same manner that you love yourself."

What does that mean? What does it <u>really</u> mean? Later, at three o'clock in the morning, I woke up hearing this phrase in my head: "Accept." At this hour, I was still a little groggy, and I said, "Wait. Accept what?" He answered, "Accept." "Okay, I'm lost. What was the conversation again?" I hear again, "Accept." Again I say, "I don't understand." Then I was reminded *"Love God, love your neighbor in the same manner you love yourself."*

"What does that mean, 'accept?'" Then I heard the rest of the conversation. "Accept without question, without reservation, without judgment." I thought, "I'm not sure that I know (again) what that means or what that looks like."

Accept another person exactly the way they are—without question, without reservation, without judgment. That is true love. It is a God kind of love. If that is love, then when I love another in the same manner as I love myself, it means that I also need to accept myself exactly where I am, the way I am, without question, reservation, or judgment.

When I talk with clients about that, I usually hear, "Well, I don't think you understand, and I don't think you know what this person has done." That's essentially the same conversation that Ananias had with God, talking about Saul. When God said go and minister to Saul, Ananias said, "I'm not really sure you understand what this man has been doing." God said, "Yes, I do, and he's a chosen vessel." There's more to the story, but the point is that even Ananias said, "Whoa, hang on a minute. I don't think you understand" (Acts 9:10–19, paraphrased).

Yes, we are to accept people without question, without reservation, and without judgment. However, I'm not asking you to stay a victim. I'm asking you to have good solid boundaries. Having good solid boundaries keeps us from walking in victimhood, and muttering, "Oh, but think about all I've done for this person, and they don't appreciate anything." Well, that just keeps us in victimhood, doesn't it?

A little side track here. Again, the best way not to be a victim is to have good healthy boundaries.[iii] Having a good solid boundary keeps us in a healthier relationship with another person. Let's say we are interacting with someone who has addictions, and they keep asking for money or something else. Can we accept that person where they are in their process? Yes. Do we have to finance it? No. Do we have to allow their poor behavior to disrupt our lives? No. Can we have boundaries with children, and obedience? Yes. Can we accept them where they are? Yes. You would not expect a small child to have the same boundaries as an older child. Can we love them while we discipline them? Absolutely.[iv]

Yes, there are healthy ways and unhealthy ways to approach any given situation. It is a learning experience to discover what works for you and what doesn't. However, today, right now, our focus is on acceptance. Not only acceptance for another person, but also acceptance for ourselves. "I give myself permission to accept myself where I am in my personal growth, in my spiritual relationships, in my person-to-person relationships, and in my life. I give myself permission to accept where I am in this moment without question, without reservation, and without judgment." Acceptance is like a gift because it allows us and others to receive a measure of compassion while at the same time holding us/them to healthier boundaries.

Don't hold back. Reservation is holding back. "Without reservation" is freely giving that acceptance rather than holding it back. Many people are so afraid that they will not be accepted for <u>who</u> they are that it creates disharmony in their lives and the lives of the people around them. Likewise, many people are afraid of being rejected. When we accept without reservation, we are giving them a gift by saying that there is no need to fear.

When we walk through the process of acceptance without judgment, then we understand that no one needs to be perfect. And this statement is coming from a recovering perfectionist! In my recovering perfectionism, I finally realized that I didn't have to do <u>everything</u> perfect. Then, one day, I realized I couldn't even do that perfect. So there was acceptance in that as well!

Eventually, we walk out of our need for perfection. Why do we feel like we need to be perfect? Because we are afraid we won't be loved. Because we are afraid we won't be accepted. The judgment comes out of fear. Usually we are our own guideline as to what is good and acceptable. We judge because we see their behavior in us, even if we don't recognize it. If we cannot accept ourselves, it is nearly impossible to truly accept another person. This is the very reason why the scripture said that we should love another person in the same manner as we love ourselves. I cannot even begin to say what a big concept this is for us to understand. Tremendous inner healing can occur if we are able to come to understand this point alone!

Accepting ourselves and others must be a daily practice, so that when we find ourselves in the midst of turmoil, in the midst of wondering how we will get through our next life lesson, we are able to accept ourselves through the process without question, without reservation, and without judgment.

Trust

It's easy to fight this process. Again, the reason that we fight or resist is fear. Although we started with love and acceptance, remember that the first opposite to fear is trust. Countless times I have heard clients tell me that it is very difficult for them to trust others. My question for them is, "Can you trust you?" Trust comes from a relationship.

Trusting God

Let's look at this another way. Jeremiah 29:11 says, "'I say this because I know what I am planning for you,' says the Lord. 'I have good plans for you, not plans to hurt you. I will give you hope and a good future.'" If I know that God has good plans for me, to give me hope and a future, then I can acknowledge that He has my best interests at heart. If I know that to be true, then I can trust that. I may not know where I'm going or how I'm going to get there, but I can trust Him. A friend once said, "When you walk in trust, it is impossible to walk in fear." Trust comes from a relationship, and trust strengthens the foundation of that relationship.

"When I am afraid, I put my trust in you" (Psalm 56:3 NIV). "I believe, Lord. Help my unbelief. I believe. Okay, I want to believe. I need a little help here. I know you have my best interests at heart. At least I think I know that. Okay. I choose to trust even if I don't know how." When we're walking in trust, we cannot be walking in fear. They're opposite. The first opposite is trust.

Trust and the Shopping Cart

I often coach clients to begin trusting themselves in the little things. Have you ever tried to decide which line at the grocery store is best? Or which route to take to work? How often have you thought one thing, only to reason your way out of it, and then realize you were right the first time?

One day I was at the store and saw a lonely shopping cart in a nearly empty parking lot. My intuitive thought was, "Better get that cart." My reasoning thought came in saying, "No one is here. All the carts must be inside. Get one in there." Reasoning won over intuition. Guess what? When I walked into the store, there were no carts. I trekked all the way to the other end of the store. Again, no carts. I thought, "I know where a cart is," and walked to the other entrance and back outside to the lonely cart. Which wasn't there. In the end, it took 20 minutes to get a cart, and I learned a valuable lesson about trusting my intuitive instincts.

After that, I started the training of trusting myself in the little things, and learned that by trusting myself in the little things, it is easier to trust myself in the big things.

"The best way to find out if you can trust somebody is to trust them." Ernest Hemingway

Truth

"I keep trying to reach the goal and get the prize for which God called me through Christ to the life above. All of us who are spiritually mature should think this way, too. And if there are things you do not agree with, God will make them clear to you" (Philippians 3:14–15 NCV).

"I give myself permission to discover, discern, and know the absolute truth." We can discover many things along our lives' journeys. It takes some discernment to determine what is absolute and what is someone's version of the truth. When we are not sure or cannot discern and know, then we can ask, "Show me the truth. I don't want anything but the absolute truth." If you come across something and you're not sure if it's true or not—or if it goes against everything that you've ever held sacred—examine it for what it is. Own it.

Know why you believe what you believe. Examine it for the truth that is in it. If there's no truth in it, that's fine. If it's niggling at you, put it on a shelf. If you're not sure if it's true but it feels like maybe it's true, put it on a shelf. Ask the question. Go back to the God session. "You know what? Here I am. I'm faced with this thing. I don't know if it's true or not. I don't want to be going down the wrong road. I don't want a rabbit chase. All I want to know is what's true. I need you to show me unequivocally what is true."

Allow God to make it clear to you. "I give God permission to make it clear to me. I give myself permission to receive clarity from God." Sometimes we resist what God is trying to do for us. Therefore, there are times when we need to give God permission. He will not intrude in our lives. Part of the reason for prayer is to partner with God in all that He has for us.

When we seek the truth, we will find the truth. God honors that. Truth is the opposite of fear. What is fear? False evidence appearing real. Truth is the opposite.

Clarity

When we understand what the truth is <u>and</u> we can trust it, we gain an amount of clarity that is unsurpassed. That clarity gives us vision. It outlines our path. Suddenly everything makes sense. Suddenly it all comes together. That is clarity. Because we have that clear vision, that clear path, because it is so well laid out in front of us, and because we've sought the truth and chosen to trust, we have that clarity—and that makes it easier to love.

Heart Code: Truth, Trust, Clarity, Love

Why is love the opposite of fear? Number one, because in love, we can accept people—and what is one of the biggest fears people have? The fear of not being accepted (or rejection, which is similar to not being accepted). "Such love has no fear, because perfect love expels all fear" 1 John 4:18 (NLT). When we operate in truth, trust, clarity, and love, we are operating in what I call a "Heart Code." There are four chambers of the heart and there are four opposites to fear. Coincidence? Maybe. Maybe not. The heart resonates with emotions, and it can change things. Having that coherence in your heart, according to HeartMath.com, can change things.

It can change your DNA (Rein 10). It can change your health. It can change your relationships (McCraty 2003 p. 7).

If we were to put truth, trust, clarity, and love into a script, what would it sound like?

"It is okay. I can give myself permission to resonate with the truth, to align my spirit, mind, will, emotions, soul, and body with the absolute truth, to trust that truth, to accept the clarity that truth brings to me so that I can love God and others in the same manner that I love myself. In doing so, I can set healthy boundaries and accept myself and others exactly the way that we are without question, without reservation, and without judgment."

In being able to walk opposite to fear and using a script that works for you, you are better able to start your healing path in a way that says, "I don't have to play the sick game. I don't have to play the disease game. I don't have to play the game that says, 'argue with people.'

"I can operate in truth, trust, clarity, and love, which brings health to my heart and healing to my soul. Bringing health and coherence to my heart allows me to walk in a measure of health that is unsurpassed." In our next section, we will explore nurturing and blessing, and what that looks like. When we can nurture and bless, we can really drive these truths home.

Section 5

Blessings

> **"Cell life molds itself from the very air we breathe, the food we eat, the thoughts and feelings we entertain and the home life we habitually live."—Bernard Jensen, author _The Science and Practice of Iridology_.**

After exploring the Heart Code and the opposites to fear, I want to take time now to discuss the heart. Often associated with the innermost part of our being, that which is at the very core of our nature, the heart is the nurturer and harmonizer of the body. Everything emanates from the heart. As we explore the heart, we will dive into some research conducted by the Institute of HeartMath. Some of this research is fairly well known, yet we will explore it anyway. First, let's introduce the "heart's field."

Heart's Field

"Compared to the electromagnetic field produced by the brain, the electrical component of the heart's field is about 60 times greater in amplitude, and permeates every cell in the body. "We propose that the heart's field acts as a carrier wave for information that provides a global synchronizing signal for the entire body. Basic research at the Institute of HeartMath shows that information pertaining to a person's emotional state is also communicated throughout the body via the heart's electromagnetic field" (McCraty Bradley and Tomasino 2004c p. 16).

Simply put, imagine the heart's field—this electromagnetic field—encircling your entire body. It emanates from the heart to the front, then to the back, and completely encompasses you in its field. Whatever is going on in the heart is being sent out and permeating every single cell. That means that no matter what happens to us physically, energetically, mentally, emotionally, or spiritually, the heart is in a continuous state of updating all the cells in the body with this information.

The heart not only updates and sends information with every heartbeat (via the bloodstream), but is also sends it out through its heart's field, similar to radio waves. "In simple terms most people can relate to, when we're having a bad day, going through a rough period such as dealing with sickness of a loved one, or coping with financial trouble, *we can actually influence our bodies—*

all the way down to the cellular level—by *intentionally thinking* positive thoughts and focusing on positive emotions" (HeartMath 2011 p. 3).

Heart Intelligence

The next thing that's really important to understand is that not only does the heart do all of that, but, as Doc Childre suggests in his heart intelligence theory, there is also an energetic connection or coupling of information between the DNA and the higher self, or the spirit (HeartMath 2011 p.2). Research shows that human intention can influence DNA (McCraty and Tomasino; HeartMath 2011). Going back, remember that we said that there's no distance in the spirit. Remember that we said that emotions play a key role in all of the heart's field's influence.

"Energetic interactions . . . occur between individuals and also affect social exchanges and relationships . . . . It appears that the heart's field plays an important role in communicating physiological, psychological, and social information *between individuals* . . . . We have been able to measure an exchange of heart energy between individuals up to five feet apart" (McCraty Bradley and Tomasino 2004c p. 17).

We are interconnected, and what we feel can actually impact each other's physiology—the physical body and its functions. Our emotions can affect someone else, and their emotions can affect us. With this in mind, imagine your heart's field surrounding you right now. It is as though your cells are continuously bathed by the heart's field (McCraty 2003 p. 15). Hence, if you feel a negative emotion, all of your cells are going to be bathed in that negative emotion. If you're feeling positive emotions, you are going to be bathed in those positive emotions.

Let me point out a concept about this interaction between the body and the field of energy that surrounds and operates it. It is almost like a holographic information processing system (McCraty, Atkinson, and Tomasino pp. 335). The idea here is that the heart's field can extend beyond you and affect the other people around you.

Since research has shown that human intention can influence DNA, I want to tell you this story I heard several years ago. There was a woman who most would view as rather average looking. Her husband adored her. Every day, he told her how beautiful she was. "Honey, you are so beautiful." Every day, he nurtured her with loving words—words he knew to be true. What happened as a result was phenomenal.

About three years later, this woman had become stunningly gorgeous. Her physical appearance changed because her husband nurtured her with his thoughts and words. He believed in his heart that she was beautiful, and he nurtured her, showering her with his words. Based on what we now know, his heart's field influenced her physical structure. Her physiology—her body—resonated with his heart's field's emotions and with the words he spoke, creating a shift in her DNA and the way that it expressed itself. We're not bound to our DNA. Our DNA is changing all the time. That is the basis of the pioneering science of epigenetics discussed by scientists like Bruce Lipton.

There is an abundance of research that supports this. Every time this man nurtured his wife, she was bathed in those loving words. Masaru Emoto has written several books about the nature of water. The crystalline structure of water can be programmed using words alone. Words can directly change the physical structure of water molecules. The human body is, by molecule, 99% water. By volume, the body is 70–90% water. Not only can water be programmed, but it also has memory. It remembers this new programming within its memory clusters formed by its crystalline structure. It is that crystalline structured water that bathes every single cell in our body.

This man blessed his wife. He blessed her every day. His heart's field affected her physiology, including her DNA. His words affected the water in her body. That water bathed all of her cells and her DNA.

What words would you like your cells bathed in?

"Think about the things that are good and worthy of praise. Think about the things that are true and honorable and right and pure and beautiful and respected" (Philippians 4:8 NCV).

Choosing to Bless

"Today, I have given you the choice between life and death. Between blessings and curses. Now, I call on heaven and earth to witness the choice you make. Oh, that you would choose life. So that you and your descendants might live" Deuteronomy 30:19 (NLT).

Blessings equal life and life equals blessings. Making the choice between blessings and curses, between life and death, was so important that Moses called on heaven and earth to witness the decision. He called on the <u>universe</u> to witness this choice so that God's people throughout generations will be able to truly understand how important these choices are. It is a monumental decision in your life to choose blessings. I encourage you to think through how you would like to be blessed, and how you can, in turn, bless others.

I would venture to say that every single one of us wants to be blessed. Blessings build our relationships. They build trust. They build us up rather than tearing us down. Blessings help us to feel better. Science is supporting the fact that conscious human intention (and the choice to bless) can actually influence the body all the way down to the structure of the cells, and it can actually help with the structure of the DNA (Rein 8; McCraty, Atkinson, and Tomasino 2004b).

Let's revisit our memory network exercises. Let's make a room that represents a complete picture of health. Think about what <u>your</u> definition of good health is. Step into that room. Allow that to be just like a warm blanket that surrounds you and comforts you, and just soak it all the way in, not only to the bones, but to every single cell in your body, even down to your DNA. In this new room, bless and nurture yourself with this new definition of health and healing for your entire body, all the way down to the smallest molecule, even into the heart's field that bathes your cells energetically and the water that bathes your cells physically.

Dimensional Aspects

We have many dimensions and facets. Most people would agree with that. My view about our dimensional aspects differs from other views: I believe there are 10 dimensions that make us what we are. Each dimension has its own unique properties. Since this is a rather extensive topic, I will discuss the 10 dimensions in detail in another book. For now, we will explore 4 of those 10 dimensions here: the physical body, the soul, the mind, will, and emotions, and the spirit.

"For the flesh desires what is contrary to the spirit, and the spirit what is contrary to the flesh. They are in conflict with each other, so that you are not to do whatever you want" Galatians 5:17 (NIV).

Often our spiritual goals conflict with our bodies. If we have been eating junk food for years, then decide to eat healthier food, the body will cry, "I am hungry!!" If we decide to start reading our Bible more, our mind, will, and emotions might rather watch our favorite program on TV. Therefore, my view of the dimensions consists of a hierarchy in which the spirit rules over the mind, will, and emotions; the mind, will, and emotions rule over the soul; the soul rules over the body; and the body is comprised of the organs, the endocrine system, the body parts, the energetic systems, and DNA. When I think of nurturing, I think of blessing each facet of <u>you</u>. I think of blessing each dimension of you.

Spirit

Let's look at each dimension separately. First, let's look at the spirit. Arthur Burk (www.TheSLG.com) has done many, many videos and audio recordings, and written many articles about the spirit and blessing the spirit. In his video *Your Spirit and Surgery*, he states that the spirit does not sleep. The spirit is immune to anesthesia because it is the spirit that is in charge (*Your Spirit and Surgery*, video; *Your Health and the Redemptive Gifts*, CD series) Now, remember, there's no distance in the spirit.

Normally, we are not really attuned to listening at the spirit level. To do so will take some fine tuning of the senses to allow us to recognize who is talking. Is it our spirit talking? Is it God talking? Is it someone else talking? Are the mind, will, and emotions talking? Is it the soul talking, or the body talking?

You know your body is talking when your shoulder is hurting. But there is a subtler difference when discerning between the spirit, the soul, and the mind, will, and emotions. Usually, the spirit is the quiet "still small voice." Our spirit's voice could be the one that wakes us up at night. In fact, if the spirit does not sleep, and is in charge, then you can ask your spirit to start taking authority and directing certain aspects of your life. For example, the spirit can give direction to your mind, will, and emotions, your soul, and your body in any healing process. If, however, the spirit is broken, then that brokenness affects all dimensions.

Body

Let's look at the dimensions from the bottom up, starting with the body. The body includes all the organs, the endocrine system, and all the body parts. Anything going on in the physical body, <u>any</u> physiological change, is going to be held and represented within this dimension of the body/mind complex.

Soul

The next dimension is the soul. This is where there can be really deep wounds. A lot of deep wounds often reside in the soul. The phrase "soul-level healing" would apply to this dimension. It is possible to have scars on your soul. If you have scars on the body, it inhibits the free flow of communication, whether it be blood, nerve, or lymph. In the same way, if you have a scar on the soul, it can inhibit communication and the growth of your soul. It can inhibit how well you feel. Often there is that soul-level wound that really affects all of the other dimensions and inhibits our healing on all dimensional levels.

Mind, Will, and Emotions

Although it does include the conscious thinking mind as well, I think of the dimension of the mind as more closely aligning with the subconscious or the unconscious mind. Just like the body and soul, the mind, will, and emotions can have wounds and scars. We have a large psychiatric community that openly discusses mental and emotional health, and how mental and emotional scars affect us. Some of those wounds are known to the conscious mind, but many are buried deep within the unconscious.

Rarely discussed within the psychiatric community is the will, will power, will to survive, and will to be your authentic self. I propose that since the mind, will, and emotions are interconnected with each other, any wound in this dimension affects all three simultaneously.

The Spirit as the Overseer

These four dimensions represent much of what we recognize as "us." Wrapping it up and overseeing it all is the spirit. I'm going to challenge you at this point to give your spirit permission to oversee your healing process. I'm going to encourage you to give your mind, your will, and your emotions permission to allow the spirit to do so. I'm going to encourage you to give your soul permission and your body permission to do the same. If, at this point, there is anything that comes to your mind that you feel you need permission for—on any of these levels—please take time to do that now.

Intentions and Blessings

All of this takes truth, trust, clarity, and love to a completely new level. Let's take a look at the conscious intentions we have towards ourselves. Knowing that our intentions can change our DNA, bless your whole being—your "whole self." Bless your body. Bless your soul. Bless your mind, will, and emotions. Bless your spirit. Instead of thinking, "Oh, I wish my body could do this or that," bless your body with the ability to heal, and bless your spirit with the ability to oversee that healing. If we focus our intentions and pay attention to how we feel when we're blessed, it radiates throughout our entire body via our heart's field and bathes our cells and DNA with those blessings.

Think about what it would mean to love another person in the same manner as you love yourself. In blessing yourself, on purpose and with purpose, you're nurturing yourself and nourishing yourself in all dimensions. You're accepting yourself exactly the way you are, even though you know there's some work to do. Now, you can translate that into a new and deeper way to love another person in the same manner that you love yourself.

Here's how it might look: "I call your spirit to attention. I call your mind, will, and emotions to attention. I call your soul to attention. I call your body to attention. To bless you. To nourish you. To see all that is good in you. I bless you with truth, trust, clarity, and love. With acceptance. I bless you with the ability to know what is true. To trust yourself in the little things, so you can trust yourself in the big things. I bless you with the ability to have clarity. Clarity of vision, clarity of focus, clarity in spirit. I bless you with the ability to love. To accept yourself and others exactly the way you are, without question, without reservation, and without judgment."

Section 6

Frequencies

Bernard Jensen, in the *Chemistry of Man*, said, "Every object on earth has a certain vibrational frequency that can destroy it completely. Opera singers can break wine glasses by hitting high notes, marching soldiers break step when crossing a bridge to avoid damaging it structurally. A plucked string on one guitar can cause the string on another guitar a few feet away to start vibrating. Is it so strange to think that a disease would have a certain vibration?" My question is, is it so strange to think that health would have a certain vibration?

Albert Einstein said, "Everything in life is vibration," and vibrations are frequencies. We hear a lot of talk about "raising your vibration" and about "changing your frequency." Think about frequencies as sound. Sound is vibration. Every single sound has a frequency. When God created the heavens and the earth, he spoke everything into existence. When he made man, he used his hands, but the very material that he used in order to make man he had already spoken into existence. The very fabric of our universe was made via sound. Sounds can create. Sounds can destroy. Words and music make you feel emotions—negative emotions or positive emotions.

Researchers are even discussing the health benefits of tuning the musical note A to 432 hertz instead of 440 hertz. "432 Hz is said to be mathematically consistent with the patterns of the universe . . . . Cymatics illustrate that when sound frequencies move through a particular medium such as water, air, or sand, they directly alter the vibration of matter" (St. Onge).

In the same way that the heart has this electromagnetic field that completely surrounds the person, Cymatics.org is showing that sound goes out not as a sine wave, but instead as a spherical shape that has its own unique geometry. In fact, when we speak, we are surrounded by this geometrical sound sphere. Sound goes out in *all* directions, not just one.

Our bodies become encased in the words that we speak.

The psalmist wrote, "Let the words of my mouth and the meditation of my heart be pleasing in your sight" (Psalm 19:14 NIV).

In other words, "Let my <u>spoken</u> words and my <u>unspoken</u> thoughts be pleasing in your sight." Spoken words are audible sound. Unspoken thoughts are inaudible sound. We hear the words of our thoughts in our minds. Those unspoken thoughts are still sound vibrations, although silent ones. The words that we say and the thoughts that we think surround us, penetrating deep into our very being. With the frequencies of the feelings emanating from the heart's field and the vibration of the words programming the water in our bodies, we *become* what we speak, think, and meditate on. As we discussed in the last section, these frequencies penetrate all the way in to our very DNA. The words we choose to say and think can make such a big difference in our health and the quality of our lives.

Years ago, when I was just out of high school, I remember a girl telling me how depressed she was. She kept singing a song from the old TV series *HeeHaw*. The song was pretty catchy. A lot of people sang it. She sang it all the time. The song was about gloom and despair. She wondered why she was depressed, so I asked her, "Do you think it could be the song you are singing?"

Early in my BodyTalk career, I did a session for a teenager who very suddenly had become afraid to sleep. He was having terrible, terrible fears of death, and was afraid that if he went to sleep, he wouldn't wake up. His mother made an appointment with an acupuncturist and an appointment with me. At his first acupuncture appointment, the acupuncturist took his pulses and said, "It may take several weeks of acupuncture sessions to help with this, and we're not really sure what's going on, but we certainly need to balance him because his system is very imbalanced."

He saw the acupuncturist the day after his BodyTalk session with me. The BodyTalk session highlighted a particular song he was listening to. That song was all about death, destruction, and killing. It was not about things that made him feel good. It was about things that made him feel bad—especially since he was singing this song quite a bit. The sound vibration of the song and the emotions he felt in his heart's field completely surrounded his entire system. His fears began adding to his anxiety, to the point that he couldn't sleep in his own room, instead choosing to make a pallet on his parent's floor.

In the session, I said, "You're going to get the mom talk and you're going to get the practitioner talk." The practitioner-side of me told him that the subconscious mind says "yes" to everything that we say or think. It takes what we are singing and it plays it forwards and backwards, and turns it upside down and begins to tumble it this way and that to try and make sense of it. (Remember the golf story?) This teenager's mind was trying to figure out how to make that song work because he was singing it so much. The mom side of me told him, "If Jesus or your subconscious mind walked around behind you and said 'Yes' to everything you said or thought, is that what you really want?" He answered with an emphatic, "NO!" So I said to him, "Change your song."

I challenge you to think about this. If Jesus walked around behind *you* and said "Yes" to everything you said or thought, is that what you'd want? If your answer is no, begin to change your words. How do you change your words? Remember the picture of what it is that you <u>do</u> want, and make your words match that picture. Any words that do not line up with that picture, "take those thoughts captive into the obedience of Christ" (2 Corinthians 10:5 KJV). There is so much power in your words, and that is the point that I want to make. "Let the words of my mouth and the meditations of my heart be pleasing in your sight." In other words, "Let my <u>spoken</u> words and my <u>unspoken</u> thoughts be pleasing in your sight." Why would the psalmist pray this? Because he knew that there is great power in our words and thoughts.

Psalm 49:3 (NIV) says, "My mouth will speak wisely and I will understand what I think about." The Holman Christian Standard Bible translates it as, "My mouth speaks wisdom. My heart's meditation brings understanding." The New Living Translation says, "For my words are wise and my thoughts are filled with insight."

If our words and thoughts are sound vibrations and those vibrations become a geometrical sphere to completely surround our entire being, and we couple that with the power of our heart's field, think about what is nurturing our spirit, mind, will, emotions, soul, and body—including every cell and all DNA. If you add emotion to that, then the heart's field amplifies it exponentially. It impacts us, but it also impacts the physiology of the other people in our lives. Our words and our thought surround us, but also surround those close to us.

Philippians 4:8 (NCV) says, "Brothers and sisters, think about the things that are good and worthy of praise. Think about the things that are true and honorable and right and pure and beautiful and respected." The New Living Translation says, "Indeed, we all make mistakes. For if we could control our tongues, we would be perfect and could also control ourselves in every other way." Proverbs 18:21 says, "The tongue has the power of life and death."

There is power in our words. Shall we choose blessings or shall we choose something else? When we set an intention to bless with our words, we begin to make a conscious change in those whom we are blessing, whether it's us or someone else.

Guilt and Shame vs. Encouragement

We all make mistakes, but the last thing that we want to do is to become overwhelmed with shame or guilt. Those are the two lowest vibrations of emotions that we can have—the two very lowest. Very often, people will attempt to control each other using shame and guilt.

"And having gathered the congregation together, they delivered the letter. When they had read it, they rejoiced because of its encouragement" (Acts 15:30b-31 NIV). The believers rejoiced because of encouraging words. When we use encouraging words, we have much better relationships. Encouraging words build trust because they bless people. Not only that, but the sounds that go forth from our mouths begin to change the DNA, and begin to change the cellular structure because we are using our words with intention (Rein 8; McCraty, Atkinson, and Tomasino 2004b).

Intention and Attention

We use <u>intention</u> when we say our words. We give <u>attention</u> to the person we are speaking to while we say those words, and our words begin to change their cellular structure. It can change it for the good or it can change it for the bad. Therefore, we want to encourage people, to build them up rather than tear them down.

For example, let's find a kind, compassionate, civil way to set boundaries. Say someone is doing something that we don't like—let's find a way to set a boundary, but use encouraging words. Maybe this person came home feeling really upset. They didn't tell us that it was a bad day, but it was clear that they were upset or in a bad mood. They may accuse those around them and find faults that are not there. Set a boundary using encouraging words such as, "I understand that maybe you had a bad day, but let's not make it personal. If you'd like to talk about what's bothering you, I'm happy to do that."

By setting those boundaries—but doing it in an encouraging way with no judgment, using truth, trust, clarity, and love; keeping your vibration at those higher levels of vibration—we are better able to build relationships and bring health and healing not only to us, but to others as well.

Notes

Section 7

Time

There was a particular event in my life where there was a speaker coming to our town and I really wanted to be able to go, but couldn't, I talked with a friend of mine and asked her to take notes for me. Even though I could not attend, I decided to do some research and study on my own, and found some profound truths that I wanted to share with my friend. I was pretty excited about some of the things that I had learned, even though I was disappointed that I couldn't go and listen to the speaker.

The next day, I called my friend to share with her what I had learned, and wanted to hear what she had learned from the speaker. As I was sharing what I was learning, my friend told me, "You know, that's exactly what we talked about last night. So you were there. You were there in the spirit, and you learned the same things that we did." That was really a pivotal moment for me. The more we want to participate in something—in this particular case, a learning event—and the more we put our focus and attention on that, the more we are there in the spirit. In this case, I focused on discovering truths, and when I decided to focus my attention on that, the truth came to me. I wanted to know what the speaker was discussing and had a general subject to focus on. In my discoveries, my friend and I found that what I learned was nearly identical to what he taught. It was my first introduction to the idea that there is no distance in the spirit.

Chronos Time and Kairos Time

In the Greek language there are two words for time: "chronos" and "kairos." Chronos is chronological time. It is the time on a calendar, and on a clock. Chronos is the time that marches on. It is linear time that moves you from one minute to the next, one second to the next, seconds upon seconds creating minutes, creating hours, creating days, creating years, and so on.

Kairos is the "right time"—an opportune moment, a supreme moment. It can be described as a season and an indeterminate time, which means that it's a moment, it's an appointed time—especially an appointed time in the purpose of God.

Distinguishing between these two different kinds of time as described in the Greek language is important, because while we live in linear time, we function very often in kairos time. We function in the <u>moment</u>. We don't usually function in the <u>minute</u>—we function in the moment. Our memories are made in the "moments" of our lives, not in the minutes of our lives.

Based on my research, I conclude that there is scientific proof that there is no distance in the spirit. Let me present the science, then we can move through it in more simplistic terms.

Mathematicians have proven that there is a universal connectivity via what they call a zero point field. This universal connectivity describes instantaneous communication. "There's always a path between two points in the space-time universe. This condition of adjacency or inseparability means that non-locality holds for both space and time. Because any two points in time can become adjacent, in effect they are inseparably entangled or interconnected." In other words, when these moments come together side-by-side and become entangled and inseparable, then there's an energetic resonance to a deeper connection whereby intuitive understanding—including spiritual insight about oneself, others, and the underlying order of the universe—is accessed. Not only that, but there can be resonant feedback looking at what would involve the brain, the heart, and the body as a whole, by which we can receive and process this information *that is not local* to where and when we are (Bradley 73, 85).

I think this research explains scientifically and mathematically why there's no distance in the spirit. Let me add this to the concept of the memory networks. Because there is no distance in the spirit, when we tune into others and put our focus, attention, and intention towards another person, we can transcend that time and space and connect directly to the other person. We can feel that person's emotions, even over a vast distance— and they can feel ours.

When they are tuning into us, we can feel their emotions. Even when they go about their day-to-day lives, we may be able to feel their emotions. Sometimes when I feel intense emotions, I will ask myself if they are my emotions, or if they belong to someone else. People who are more sensitive to emotions, like empathic people, tend to feel other people's emotions rather strongly. It's always a good idea to ask whether or not it is your emotion that you're feeling—especially if it's anxiety or fear. That's what I do. Tension in a room would be a good example, since you can feel the tension even if you are completely separate from the situation.

Communication Channels

The HeartMath research shows that the communication channels bring us all together. They connect us into that one body that we talked about. In the same way that we have one body that's made of many parts and the entire body knows when you bang your little toe, sometimes when we have a deep emotional connection with someone we can have their same experiences. This is something we haven't really been able to understand prior to some of this research, yet before I found the research I experienced it in my own life with my family members and with friends.

I would have this feeling of an emotion that wasn't my emotion, and I would stop and ask, "Whose emotion is this?" And I would wait until I had a clear understanding about who it belonged to, and then I would contact that person and ask, "Are you doing okay?" Then I would find out why I was actually feeling that emotion, because they would begin to tell me what was going on. Let me bring this back down a bit.

I want to look at time, and I want to look at a function of time, which is rhythm. One of the basic premises of HeartMath is that there are clear rhythmic patterns in the beat-to-beat heart rate (McCraty 2003 1). Much of the HeartMath research discusses this heart rhythm, and the variability of the heart rhythm. The heart is the harmonizer in the body, and rhythm is a function of time. I propose that this heart rhythm is also a function of time, and allows the heart to communicate outside space and time. There is an inter-connectedness that we all have with each other via our hearts, and this is part of the idea of there being no distance in the spirit.

Interconnectedness Through Kairos Moments of Memories

When we think back on a memory, we are connecting the kairos moment of "now" to the kairos moment of the event. We are transported through time and space to that moment. In a sense, we are time-traveling to that moment. The more emotional we are about an event—especially if there are negative emotions—the more stuck in that moment we get, the more *stuck in time* we get. Why? Because all of those kairos moments line up with each other, so we are interconnecting and entangling many kairos moments together. *This* moment that you think about the memory becomes entangled to *that* moment when you thought about the memory, to all of the other moments when you thought about the memory, to the moments when you go to bed at night thinking about the memory, and on and on.

Based on the mathematical science, I propose that all those many "separate" kairos moments become interconnected and entangled, and become one big kairos moment in time that is focused on that memory. They are no longer separate moments. They are ONE moment with no distance in the spirit.

When we understand this, we can use our memory network technique from Section 2. We can go to that event; look at it through all kairos time, and clear the memory through all time and space. In other words, we can clear all of the kairos moments as though it is one kairos moment, because it is. And because it is one kairos moment—there's only the one instance to clear—this can potentially remove the time barriers to healing (whether it's healing for the spirit, the mind, will, emotions, soul, or the body).

Essentially, if we only clear the initial moment of the event without clearing all the other moments that we thought about the event, then it would be like picking up large pieces of broken glass but leaving the tiny glass dust behind.

I think it is our heart rhythm that connects us to an infinite God and his divine time, giving us the ability to heal across space and time. We have the ability to live in chronological linear time, while also living *and healing* in divine time (the kairos time).

Let's work through the memory network exercise now. What I would like for you to do is to think back to any of the exercises that you have done on memory networks from Section 2 that may still be lingering with you. I want you to go back and do the exercise again, but this time focus your attention on connecting all of those kairos moments when you relived the event or felt the emotions.

Imagine all those kairos moments connecting together into one big moment through all space and time. In fact, you could even imagine that you are connecting to all of the places on the earth where you were while thinking about the event. You may not remember every single moment. It is highly unlikely that you would, but you <u>can</u> imagine that all those moments are interconnected and become one big moment. That is our focus: the one big kairos moment that represents every time we experienced or thought about the event.

I think of a big ball—a Kairos Ball—that holds all this together for me. Or I think of the room we used in the memory network exercise to hold it all together. Now that you have the focus for kairos time, focus on the space—the physical locations that you were in—and add those to the kairos ball or kairos room for the event.

When you work through the memory network exercise, with this big understanding of kairos time, and you can think about all of those moments coming together in one big ball, you can clear the memories through all time and space. Connect with the people again if necessary, through time and space. In other words, we are not only connecting to the past, but we're connecting to the future too (via kairos moments when someone in a future time might think about the memory or event).

We're connecting all of those entangled moments together so that there can be healing for everyone who has ever been involved directly or by thinking on it. Then I want you to sit with what we have just done. I want you to think about how this new healing feels. Continue with the exercise until you have a peace that surpasses all understanding. Continue with it until you know that it's complete.

Contemplation

You may need to contemplate this section, because there's a lot of information that I've given you. You may want to set the information on a virtual shelf to revisit later. It may take some prayer, and it may take some meditating, which is the act of deep thinking and consideration (Philippians 4:6–9). Think about it— think out loud. Put some thought into the truths that are coming to your awareness.

When you're comfortable with it, then you can go back to the memory network exercise and work on that memory and event with the new consideration of kairos time. You can accomplish a healing that has not been accomplished before. When you release the other people from the memory—when you release yourself from the memory—you are releasing the memory through all time and space. You're releasing it through divine time. You are releasing the moments spent contemplating and reliving the memory, which then brings a more complete balancing of it.

Remember to bless the others in the memory. You're blessing them through all time and space. You're blessing them through divine time. You're connecting this moment of blessing to all moments of blessing. Send those blessings into that one big kairos moment, and bless across all time and space. See how that feels. Continue to think through it, and continue to see how else you can utilize this new concept of time in moments of your life.

Notes

Section 8

Freedom in Your Hands

Freedom is in your hands now because you have techniques that give you an ability to release those things that have kept you from attaining whole health.

Strongholds

Strongholds are mighty fortresses. In ancient times, the walls of fortresses were many feet thick. They protected castles and strong walled cities. Nothing could get through those walls. Our wounds are strongholds that resonate with memories and negative emotions, the most deadly of which is fear, since it opposes truth, trust, clarity, and love.

"The Lord is my light and my salvation. Whom shall I fear? The Lord is the stronghold of my life. Of whom shall I be afraid?" (Psalm 27:1 NIV).

In the same manner as we can have negative strongholds, we can have positive ones. The Lord is our stronghold. His perfect love casts out our fears (1 John 4:18). His truth shines a light so that we are freed from falsehoods. Clarity brings discernment, and our relationship with ourselves and God builds trust.

Knowing this, we can build strongholds in our lives based on these principles. We can create a sense of safety and security that perhaps we may or may not have felt in the past. 1 Peter 5:7 (NIV) says, "Cast all anxiety on him because he cares for you," or "Give your worries and your cares to God, for he cares about you" (NLT).

Worry and Anxiety

Worry is over-thinking. Sometimes people "worry" through their problems. Excessive worry leads to confusion. Anxiety is a hybrid emotion born of worry and fear.

Letting Go in Order to Receive

A pastor once took his congregation through an exercise. He said, "Place your open hands in front of you, palms up. In your hands are all your burdens and cares. Now turn your open hands face down. When your hands are face down, you cannot hold on to those burdens any longer. They are now at the feet of God. Now turn your hands over, palms up. With your burdens gone, you now have room to receive the blessings that God has for you."

The Story of the Sand

Let's imagine we are at a beach with lots of soft sand. Scoop some sand up into your hand and hold it. Imagine that you want to hold on to the sand so that it won't blow away. The sand will be a souvenir of your trip to the beach, but you have no container in which to place it. What happens if you begin to close your hand tightly around it? Tightening your hand will actually squeeze the sand out of your hands—the tighter you squeeze your hand, the more the sand flows out from the sides of it. Now, in your imagination, open your hand. How much sand is left? Very little.

Now let's imagine scooping up the sand again. This time, gently cup your hands so that you create a protection from the wind so all the sand doesn't blow away. Perhaps you place your other hand slightly over the sand to further shield it from the wind. Maybe a few grains blow away, but you're not going to lose as much as if you tried to hold the sand tightly.

Holding on. The Need for Control.

Imagine now that, instead of sand, we are trying to hold on to something we are afraid we might lose. Think about what that might be for you. What do you try to hold on to so tightly because you're afraid that you might lose it?

This fear of loss can create the need to control. If we're afraid we're going to lose something, then sometimes we move into the need to control the situation, and even to control other people. Why do we do that? Well, it could be a fear for safety. We may want to be safe. We may want our kids to be safe.

Survival Mechanisms

The need for control is a survival mechanism. Control is born of fear. There are healthy fears, which I describe as a healthy respect for something, such as heights. It is a good thing to have a healthy respect for heights, but the fear of heights can be more like a phobia. A healthy respect of heights allows you to look out the window of a tall building unafraid, but grateful that there's a wall or a window there to keep you safe. But someone who really, truly has a pathological fear of heights may not want to even go up the elevator—or if they happen to be in a building on a high floor, they may not want to be in a room that has a window.

There are many types of survival mechanisms that we use to keep ourselves safe. Some become engrained as part of our behavior because of what I call "victim mode" or "victim mentality." "Well, it's not my fault" or "Why do I get blamed for everything?" or "Why does it always have to be my fault?" When we are stuck in this victim mentality, then it is very easy to feel the need to control everything and everyone around us. Victim mentality brings a thought process to us in which we feel blamed for everything, or we attempt to throw blame onto someone else so we can stay safe. While in victim mode, we stay on the defensive continually.

What I tell my clients is, "I'm not here to help you stay a victim. I'm here to help you move through this so that you can gain victory." When we have unhealthy survival mechanisms, sometimes we have expectations that we project out into our environments.

If we expect someone to yell at us every time they see us, then that person may walk into the room and say "hello" very calmly, yet we will still perceive it as shouting. We perceive their tone as though they are yelling at us, and then we escalate it by saying, "Why do you always yell at me?" They may be surprised enough by that outburst to decide to walk out of the room and re-walk back in so that perhaps the perception can change, because all they said was hello. Through our expectations—because we expect a particular outcome—we perceive something in our environment that may not be accurate. "I give myself permission to perceive my environment as it truly is."

We focus much of our attention on what we need to do to stay safe, especially as it pertains to our relationships—whether it's the people in our family, the people at work, or people at school. You may feel unsafe in specific ways, thinking, "Well, don't get too close, because they might leave too" or "Don't get too close, they might betray me" or "Why do I always have a boss that does this?" or "Why do I always have co-workers that do that?" or "My family members never understand me." Whatever those expectations are, we begin to create what we perceive as safety mechanisms, and begin to worry quite a bit over those things.

As we begin to give ourselves permission, clear the memories, look at truth, trust, clarity, and love, look at blessing other people and ourselves, and work through this process, things are going to begin to change because our perception is going to change. When our perceptions change, the way we react to other people is going to change, and then the way they react to us is going to change.

What do you worry over? What do you feel you need to control? Remember, worry and fear create anxiety. What are the opposites of fear and anxiety? The heart code of truth, trust, clarity, and love. They alleviate and push back at the fear. The more we fill ourselves with truth, trust, clarity, and love, the easier it is to walk in that heart code, and the less room there is for the fears and anxieties—which leads me to our next concept.

Tending Someone Else's Garden

Let's say my neighbor and I both have gardens, and that I tend my garden diligently. But I notice that my neighbor's garden isn't as neat as mine. How do you think that neighbor would feel if I hopped the fence to tend a garden that wasn't mine? Not great, I would say. Crossing a boundary, I would say.

We've talked about the fears that we have about ourselves and our lives. But sometimes we have fears about other people, and we may even try to control situations for another person because we're afraid for that person. Maybe it's because we don't agree with their life choices—we don't like the way they tend their garden. If we're talking about our children, it could be that we don't like the way that they study, or we think that they could make better choices in friends, etc. Sometimes we try to control rather than setting good healthy boundaries, or because we don't know how to set healthy boundaries. We may try to control their lives because we're not willing to allow them their own autonomy and free will.

Non-Judgment

Remember that if we're judging the way that someone is living their life—and they could be children or adults, friends or family members—the judgment comes from fear. There is a reason that the scripture says, "Judge ye not, lest ye be judged. In the same manner you judge, you will be judged" (Matthew 7:1). That's the reason we don't want to judge. We want to approach this from a standpoint of truth, trust, clarity, and love—accepting someone exactly the way they are without question, without reservation, and without judgment. So instead of approaching that person with an attitude of fear, come to them with truth, trust, clarity, and love.

If we set healthy boundaries, we can encourage the people around us to gain wisdom through experience. I once heard a pastor say, "The one decision you can never make for another person, not even your children, is the decision of faith. It can only come from within that person. You cannot make a spiritual decision for any other person than you." What you <u>can</u> do is bless others with a heart code of truth, trust, clarity, and love across all kairos moments: the past, present, and future.

Take the kairos space that holds all those moments where you've worried over someone, and instead clear your worries and fears that may have been projected towards them, and then create a space for them to be able to learn and grow.

The Gift of Creating a Space

If I want to play the piano, I need to be able to have a space where I can practice, whether it's a room with only a piano and nothing else, or whether I carve out a little space in another room. Either way, I need a space with a piano or a keyboard in order to be able practice and learn to play the piano. In like manner, we can create a space in our imagination where our loved ones can walk in truth, trust, clarity, and love—to walk in that heart code of "Love God and love your neighbor as yourself." We can create the space for acceptance for who they are as individuals created by a loving God. By creating that space for them, they can choose to walk in that space, or to be in that space on their own. They maintain their own autonomy. They maintain their free will.

I can have a space to play the piano, but if I don't go to that space, I won't play the piano. We can bless them with the space, but we can't force them to walk in that space. Having the space there and available, manifested by our actions and attitudes towards them, having cleared our own stuff, gives them an opportunity that they might not have had otherwise. Operating in judgment takes that space away from them. Operating in heart code gifts them with the space they need. Whether they choose to unwrap the gift is up to them.

What does this look like? If all of these worries that we have about another person coalesce into one big kairos ball of worry that affects us across all ages, then we can give our worries and cares to God because he cares for us, and with Him, we can co-create that space of peace that surpasses all understanding.

I invite you to do a God session as we did in Section 3. In this space, present your request to God. Tell Him what you think. Tell Him how you feel. This time, go to the room that has the big kairos of all the moments that you've worried over a particular problem in your life. There's a space for "all the people in your life," and a space for "each person" in your life. In this particular area of your life, bring all those moments together, and turn your hands over, giving everything to God with truth, trust, clarity, and love—and with thanksgiving, understanding that there is wisdom to be gained from the experience. Let that thankfulness and peace wash over you. Ask for direction. Ask for clarity. Even if you don't know how.

If there's forgiveness to be received, give yourself permission to receive it. If there's forgiveness to be given—even to yourself—be willing to give it. Or perhaps give yourself permission to give it. Move out of your woundedness and into that healing space. Make the request, and turn it all over; leave nothing behind. Gather it all up into the big kairos ball so that you know you have been heard, and that the answer is on its way. Then let go of the need to know the outcome. Yes, that's easier said than done. Yes, it takes practice. But it is immensely rewarding. "Here you go, God, I'm going to let you take care of this."

The clarity that we gain from this could be the vision of the new direction to take. We may be able to know a general direction, but not the exact destination—and that's okay. Trust is putting one foot in front of the other. The freedom that you have here is a freedom that's in your hands. It's a freedom that you can hold on to, not in tightness (that would confuse the issue), but in a trust that allows you to understand a much bigger picture.

Section 9

Generational Freedom

In this section we're going to be talking about groups rather than individuals. The focus is more on generational lines, but it applies to other groups as well. The first thing that I want to discuss is collective belief systems. We've talked about our own personal belief systems, but what about those belief systems that we inherit from the community at large, from the world, or even from our families? One of these terms is called "consensus reality," which ultimately boils down to the world in which we live being defined by beliefs that are determined by a group of people, such as the community or your family. Because so many different people believe it to be so, whatever it is then remains unchallenged as a fact.

It takes a bit of discernment to determine which are straight facts (such as "the sun rises in the east") and which are seemingly true statements (such as, "there's always a line at the ladies' room"). I remember taking a class with Dr. Veltheim, founder of the International BodyTalk Association, and there was quite a lengthy discussion in the class about this collective belief system, or the "consensus reality." During a break, everyone made a rush to the restroom. I walked in and said, "Oh, there's a line." And someone said, "Well, isn't there always a line in the ladies' room?" I said, "So you're telling me the consensus reality is that there's always a line in the ladies' room," and everyone started laughing.

What I was really saying is, if everyone believes that there's always a line in the ladies' room, there will always be a line in the ladies' room. Doesn't that go back to the projected expectations that we have? If we believe it to be true, then we will prove over and over again how it *is* true. It's important to challenge these belief systems. Group belief systems can be challenged, and some have been. One of those belief systems we have begun to challenge is that we are victims of our genes. Bruce Lipton's work has proven this belief to be false. In his groundbreaking work *Biology of Belief*, we learned that we are not victims of our genes—there are other factors that can impact how our genes express themselves.

His work proved what we knew years ago: that our emotions and our belief systems, the way we think, the way we feel, those things that we hold sacred, whether religious or otherwise, can impact how our DNA expresses itself.

Over the course of many, many years, I have heard people list various complaints about their health. They list all the different people in the family who had a particular disease—whether it was that their family members all died of heart attacks or had high blood pressure, diabetes, or even something else. When they're telling their story, they usually start or end with the belief system that they too will have this issue, and that it's inevitable for them. That is not the reality.

"We are not victims to our genes." Bruce Lipton

The true reality that we live in is that our genes are mutable. One of the things that Dr. Lipton was introducing to us was the field of epigenetics, which is described as the genes on top of our genes. These are the "markers" that tell our genes how to express themselves. There can be markers to turn a gene on and there can be markers to turn a gene off.

In a policy briefing of the early origins of diabetes, the International Diabetes Federation defined epigenetics as the study of changes in gene activity that do not involve alterations to the genetic code, but still get passed down to at least one successive generation. In essence, it is the genes on top of the genes. Many factors can create markers to turn genes on or off, making our genes mutable. As Bruce Lipton states, "We are not victims to our genes."

Predispositions

When you go to the doctor, you fill out an intake form. Doctors want to know what physical and mental illnesses run in your family. They're looking for things such as heart attack or high blood pressure, diabetes, depression, cancer, and a host of other disease processes. One of the things that's important to note is that they're looking for what runs in the family—what runs on the genetic line—because they're still often looking at whether or not we have a genetic predisposition towards a particular disease. My phrasing has changed from, "What's on the DNA?" to "What is a potential, but may or may not come to pass?"

Not only do I ask those same questions when I'm speaking with a client, but I also consider other factors, such as the way we think and the belief systems that we hold. I listen to what people say. Yes, I may look at predispositions toward alcoholism and other addictions, as well as traits that may need balancing, like stubbornness, standoffishness, fear of rejection, and a myriad of others. I just listen to the client to see what patterns are present that can be addressed. Many times, these are addressed very successfully. Our focus is in healing the negatives so that the positives can come forward: friendliness, faith, joy, gifts, and talents, just to name a few.

Numbers 14:18 (NLT) says, "The Lord is slow to anger and filled with unfailing love, forgiving every kind of sin and rebellion. But he does not excuse the guilty. He lays the sins of the parents upon their children; the entire family is affected—even children in the third and fourth generations."

While this was said in the Bible millennia ago, research is now showing that illnesses such as diabetes and heart conditions can correlate back to the epigenetic factors of ancestral diet. Even though that may not be deemed a sin, it is still something that is passed down to the second, third, and fourth generations. In other words, the foods that our ancestors ate or the famine that they were exposed to could indeed impact the health of future generations, sometimes even four generations later.

Further research has shown that emotions such as fear and even disorders such as PTSD can have epigenetic implications, and that those fears can be passed down through multiple generations (Bygren, Tinghog et al; Policy Briefing Early Origins; Yehuda, Halligan and Bierer; Parsons and Ressler).

Let me repeat, though, that we are not victims of our genes. Everything is mutable. Things don't have to be the way they have been for generations just because the consensus or the community believes that that's the way that it is. We are co-creators with Christ. Everything can affect the DNA, both for good and bad.

We can use the heart code from Section 4, and use truth, trust, clarity, love, and our intentions to begin a healing process on the DNA. Isaiah 53:4–5 (NCV) says, "But he took our suffering on him and felt our pain for us. We saw his suffering and thought God was punishing him. But he was wounded for the wrong we did; he was crushed for the evil we did. The punishment, which made us well, was given to him, and we are healed because of his wounds."

Galatians 3:13 (NLT) says, "But Christ has rescued us from the curse pronounced by the law. When he was hung on the cross, he took upon himself the curse for our wrongdoing. For it is written in the Scriptures, 'Cursed is everyone who is hung on a tree.'"

Permit me to note that the Old Testament Law would have these things passed down generation to generation, and yet in the New Testament it says, "We're not bound by that law anymore. We are new creations in Christ, and we're not part of that law anymore." When it says "Cursed is everyone who is hung on a tree," that was a common phrase for the cross. By Jesus hanging on the cross, he took these things upon him, and they were transmuted away from what could be, and into what is. We have this ability to change our DNA scripturally as well as scientifically.

Permissions for Others

Before we move to healing for the generations, let's take another look at permissions. Sometimes it's important for us to let someone know "I'm thinking about you and praying for you." Or, if someone says, "I need you to pray for me," we can ask them what they want prayer for, and then stick to that. Or we can say, "How about if I pray the highest, best good for you and all involved so that you can move through this much more quickly?"

There are varying ways to do that, but the thing that we don't want to do is to use prayer as a form of manipulation and control that turns into a form of witchcraft, where we're trying to change the situation into something that suits what <u>we</u> think is okay, but what isn't necessarily the best thing for all those involved.

Anytime that we start moving into, "Oh Lord, make them do such and such," we're immediately moving into a manipulating and controlling role. We're moving into a situation of "This is what I'm asking you for, because this is what's good for me (but not necessarily what's good for the other person)."

Healing for the Generations

Let's put everything we've done in the past sections together for our generational lines and/or for the groups to which we belong. For while we have generational lines, we also have groups to which we belong, such as families, groups of friends, associations, churches, schools, businesses, and many other types of institutions.

Perhaps we can look at any of the memory events that you worked on from Section 2. Does that type of event follow your family line? Is it one of those things where you say, "This happens to every second child born" or "This happens to every girl in the family?"

Look at the event (or trait) and see if you notice a pattern in the generational lines. Look at it from a generational perspective. Are there multiple patterns you notice? Are there things that follow each generation, or are there things that skip generations? Then I will ask whether you need to give any permission to yourself or to your DNA to balance this portion of the event/memory/trait? Do you need any permission for the family line to heal spiritually, emotionally, mentally, and physically from what may have happened with past influences in the generations before you?

If you know of a particular event or a series of events in the generational line, then you can look at those events and imagine all of those who would have been present, and begin to remove your energy from those events. You can bless those involved with the ability to do the same thing—that they, too, can remove their energy. They may have passed on, but remember that in kairos, all of those moments come together and everyone is affected and impacted by the event. Thus, everyone can be impacted by what we do here. It may not make a difference for a person who has already passed, but it certainly can make a difference for all of those who are still living and still connected. In other words, there may be other generational lines that descend from that past person.

Can you bless the people who were involved in those events with the ability to pull their energy away and heal? Can you bless those who came before you in past generations? Can you bless them with truth, trust, clarity, and love? As you put all of those moments together and they become one kairos moment where everyone in the generations is feeling the impact of the event, can you allow the healing to occur across all time and space? Can you allow this space, even for your own body, soul, mind, will, emotions, and spirit? Can you allow a space for the others involved to receive healing? And can you follow that through the lines of your family and the past generations, and even going forward into future generations?

What has just been cleared for you and your family lines stops here with you. It no longer has to follow the generational lines to your children or grandchildren, or any of your descendants farther down your family line. Anyone coming after you can be blessed to never have it show up in their epigenetic markers at all. Those genes don't have to turn on or off. For your descendants, those markers don't have to dictate how the future generations' DNA is expressed.

Adoption

We all have physical, energetic, and spiritual DNA. But not all that we inherit comes through our physical bloodline DNA. If you were adopted, or if you are from a blended family, then you have a unique blend of the physical, energetic, and spiritual DNA that you inherited from your birth parents and the energetic and spiritual DNA of those who raised you. You have a unique opportunity to follow the same steps to clear the generational lines for all of your DNA from each inherited line.

Teachers and Mentors

Since we inherit from others besides those in our physical bloodline, I want to point out that if we have a mentor or a spiritual teacher, they participate in our personal, energetic, and spiritual growth, and potentially even our soul growth. They can impact those same dimensional aspects of our DNA.

As you look at what may have been inherited from those mentors and teachers, is there anything that needs to be addressed? Any behavior traits that are unique to them? Any patterns that you see in yourself that you may have inherited? I invite you to allow yourself to follow these steps to clear your spiritual DNA and the energetic DNA that was part of that spiritual inheritance. In essence, we have many, many areas where we can inherit memories, emotions, and general lines of thinking, such as consensus realities.

By broadening our approach to not just what has happened in our lives, but also to the patterns of behavior in those who came before us, and find a way to heal that. Not only are we healing it for us, but we are extending that healing to those who are still living and those who will come after. This healing may not cover those specific things that each individual needs to learn for themselves. We must be aware that they maintain their autonomy. However, by our clearing of the generational lines, they are freed from the common traits shared on that generational line, which they may or may not have inherited. If they have inherited what has been cleared, then they now have a platform for success so they can then look at their own issues to heal.

Conclusion

My hope is that, of all the tools in this work, the tool you use the most is one of your own conversation with God. I walk throughout my day asking, "Ok, God. Where are we going, and what are we doing?" It is a continual conversation. Everything I have given you first comes from asking the questions and waiting for the answers. Some of the answers, I discovered along the way. Some of the answers came from research that I found, or research that found me. Regardless of how the information came to me, I took it, prayed over it, and tested it. If it tested true, you see it here. If it did not, I left it behind.

My hope is that I have given you new ways of approaching life, health, and relationships. The reality is that everything comes down to relationships. We have relationships with everyone and everything in our environment. The healthier a relationship that we have with ourselves, the healthier our interactions with that environment will be.

DNA can be changed. Everything in our world vibrates with frequencies. Research shows us that the frequencies of our words, thoughts, and emotions can change our DNA for the worse or for the better.

Our DNA is changing all the time.

**"We are not victims to our genes"
(Bruce Lipton).**

How will you change your DNA?

Will you give yourself permission? Will you release memory themes, emotional themes, and memory networks? Will you spend time in a God Session? Will you release fear and walk in the heart code of truth, trust, clarity, and love? Will you take authority over negative thinking and allow the frequencies of feel-good emotions to permeate into your heart's field to nurture and bless your very being all the way into your cells and farther into your DNA, knowing that what is in your heart's field affects not only you, but also those who are close to you? Will you allow the healing to occur in all dimensions of you, and throughout all the kairos moments of divine time—past, present, future—and across the generations well beyond your time here on earth, blessing your descendants with abundance in health spiritually, physically, mentally, and emotionally?

My hope is that the material in this book becomes a resource for you to use over and over, not only for yourself, but for others in your life. If I could bless you now, I bless you with the ability to walk in truth, trust, clarity, and love, which brings health and coherence to your heart and allows you to walk in a measure of peace and health that is unsurpassed.

Thank You For Reading My Book!

I would love to hear your comments about the book, and how it has impacted your life.

Click into Amazon.com to leave a helpful review. Every comment is appreciated and will help the next version and the next book be even better.

If you would like more information about any of the techniques and are interested in taking a seminar, please email us at seminars@kathrynspringman.com.

Thanks so much!!

Notes

References

Aird, Kishori. (2006). Essence. (Rose-Anne Chabot & Françoise McNeil, Trans). Lithia Springs, GA: New Leaf Distributing Company.

Bradley, R. T. (2007). The Psychophysiology of Intuition: A Quantum-Holographic Theory of Nonlocal Communication. World Futures, 63(2), 61–97. http://doi.org/10.1080/02604020601123148

Burk, Arthur. (2009-2011). Blessing Your Spirit Series (CD and audio download). http://www.TheSLG.com

Burk, Arthur. (2009-2011a). Nurturing Your Spirit Series (CD and audio download). http://www.TheSLG.com

Burk, Arthur. (2011). Tools for Cleansing Time and Land. (CD and audio download). http://www.TheSLG.com

Burk, Arthur. (2012). Trauma Bonds to Time. (CD and audio download). http://www.TheSLG.com

Burk, Arthur. (2012a). Your Health and the Redemptive Gifts. (CD and audio download). http://www.TheSLG.com

Bygren, L. O., Tinghög, P., Carstensen, J., Edvinsson, S., Kaati, G., Pembrey, M. E., & Sjöström, M. (2014). Change in paternal grandmothers' early food supply influenced cardiovascular mortality of the female grandchildren. BMC Genetics, 15(1), 12–6. http://doi.org/10.1186/1471-2156-15-12

Caldecourt, Megan. (2012). The Dynamics of Time. (CD and audio download). http://www.GoBeyondTheHorizon.com

Callaway, E. (2013). Fearful memories haunt mouse descendants. Nature News. (Web) http://doi.org/10.1038/nature.2013.14272

Decker, Ed. (2015). Rollin McCraty: Closing the Gap Between Heart and Brain. (Web). http://www.rewireme.com/explorations/rollin-mccraty-closing-gap-heart-brain/

Dias, B. G. & Ressler, K. J. (2013). Parental olfactory experience influences behavior and neural structure in subsequent generations. Nature Neuroscience, 17(1), 89–96. http://doi.org/10.1038/nn.3594

Epstein, D. (n.d.). How an 1836 Famine Altered the Genes of Children Born Decades Later. (Web). http://io9.com/how-an-1836-famine-altered-the-genes-of-children-born-d-1200001177

Fosar, G. & Bludorf, F. (2011, July 12). Scientists Prove DNA Can Be Reprogrammed by Words and Frequencies | Wake Up World. (Web). http://wakeupworld.com/2011/07/12/scientist-prove-dna-can-be-reprogrammed-by-words-frequencies/

Franckh, Pierre. (2014). The DNA Field and the Law of Resonance, Creating Reality Through Conscious Thought. (Aida Sefic Williams, Trans). Rochester, VT: Destiny Books.

Harold, S. (2014, February 19). A shock of change felt down the generations—On Biology (Web). http://blogs.biomedcentral.com/on-biology/2014/02/20/a-shock-of-change-felt-down-the-generations/

HeartMath Institute. (2010, July 21). The Energetic Heart Is Unfolding—HeartMath Institute. (Web). https://www.heartmath.org/articles-of-the-heart/science-of-the-heart/the-energetic-heart-is-unfolding/

HeartMath Institute. (2011, July 13). You Can Change Your DNA—HeartMath Institute. (Web). https://www.heartmath.org/articles-of-the-heart/personal-development/you-can-change-your-dna/

Hughes, V. (2013, November 15). Mice Inherit the Fears of Their Fathers. (Web). http://phenomena.nationalgeographic.com/2013/11/15/mice-inherit-the-fears-of-their-fathers/

Klengel, T., Mehta, D., Anacker, C., Rex-Haffner, M., Pruessner, J. C., Pariante, C. M., et al. (2012). Allele-specific FKBP5 DNA demethylation mediates gene–childhood trauma interactions. Nature Neuroscience, 16(1), 33–41. http://doi.org/10.1038/nn.3275

Leonard, C. (2008, April 23). An Overview of How Stress Kills and How to Develop Your StresSkills. (Web).
http://www.naturalnews.com/023088_stress_body_emotion.html

McCraty, J. J. (2001). Local and nonlocal DNA USPA, 1–6.
https://appreciativeinquiry.case.edu/uploads/Heart Math%20article.pdf

McCraty, J. J. (2003). The Energetic Heart, 1–22.

McCraty, R., Atkinson, M., & Bradley, R. T. (2004a). Electrophysiological Evidence of Intuition: Part 1. The Surprising Role of the Heart, 1–12.
https://www.heartmath.org/assets/uploads/2015/01/intuition-part1.pdf

McCraty, R., Atkinson, M., & Bradley, R. T. (2004b). Electrophysiological Evidence of Intuition: Part 2. A System-Wide Process?, 1–12.
https://www.heartmath.org/assets/uploads/2015/01/intuition-part2.pdf

McCraty, R., Bradley, R. T., & Tomasino, D. (2004c). The Resonant Heart, 15-19.
https://www.heartmath.org/assets/uploads/2015/01/the-resonant-heart.pdf

McCraty, R., Atkinson, M., & Tomasino, D. (2003). Modulation of DNA Conformation by Heart-Focused Intention, 1–6. http://www.aipro.info/drive/File/224.pdf

Parsons, R. G., & Ressler, K. J. (2013). Implications of memory modulation for post-traumatic stress and fear disorders. Nature Neuroscience, 16(2), 146–153. http://doi.org/10.1038/nn.3296

Pert, Candice. (1999). Molecules of Emotion: The Science Behind Mind-Body Medicine. New York, NY: Simon & Schuster.

Policy_Briefing_EarlyOrigins.pdf. (n.d.). Policy_Briefing_EarlyOrigins.pdf. idf.org. https://www.idf.org/sites/default/files/Policy_Briefi ng_EarlyOrigins.pdf

Rein, G., PhD. (1996, October). Effect of Conscious Intention on Human DNA. http://www.item-bioenergy.com/infocenter/consciousintentionondna.p df

Seller, S. (n.d.). 50 years of DNA research turned upside down as scientists discover second programming language within genetic code—Sott.net. (Web). http://www.sott.net/article/270045-50-years-of-DNA-research-turned-upside-down-as-scientists-discover-second-programming-language-within-genetic-code

St.-Onge, E. (2013, December 21). Here's Why You Should Consider Converting Your Music to A=432 Hz. (Web). http://www.collective-evolution.com/2013/12/21/heres-why-you-should-convert-your-music-to-432hz/

Stone, Robert B. (1989). The Secret Life of Cells, 1-192. Atglen, PA: Schiffer Publishing Ltd.

Yehuda, R., Halligan, S. L., & Bierer, L. M. (2002). Cortisol levels in adult offspring of Holocaust survivors: relation to PTSD symptom severity in the parent and child. Psychoneuroendocrinology, 27(1-2), 171–180. http://eutils.ncbi.nlm.nih.gov/entrez/eutils/elink.fcgi?dbfrom=pubmed&id=11750777&retmode=ref&cmd=prlinks

Endnotes

[i]Arthur Burk has done much research and released many audios and videos on the spiritual dynamics of both time and land. *Trauma Bonds to Time* and *Tools for Cleansing Time and Land* are but two of these. His discussions on cleansing time are also intermingled throughout other works as well.

[ii]BreakThrough is a great class in the International BodyTalk System and available at www.BodyTalkSystem.com that takes this subject to a much deeper level. Honestly, I can't imagine doing this kind of personal growth work or conducting any BodyTalk sessions without having taken this class.

[iii]Cloud and Townsend have an entire series of books on boundaries that I recommend on a regular basis.

[iv]Kevin Leman has several excellent parenting books that I recommend. The first is *Making Children Mind Without Losing Yours*.

Notes

Appendix

Large format color versions of all illustrations are available in the Bonus Materials.

Free copies of these illustrations are available by visiting www.KathrynSpringman.com.

5 Emotional Themes

Theme	Out of Balance		In Balance	
Anger	Angry Animosity Displeasure Distrust Enraged Frustrated	Hostility Ill temper Indecisive Irritable Irritated Mad	Benevolance Decisive Forgiving Inner seeing Kindness Merciful	Movement Passionate Peace Pleasure Supported Trust
Joy Sadness	Agony Arrogance Boredom Depression Despair Disoriented	Gloom Harsh Hyper Judgmental Lack of discernment Manic	Cheerfulness Comforted Discernment Gracious Gratified Happy	Harmonious Jovial Jubilation Peace Sense of well-being Tender
Worry	Anxiety (from worry) Burdened Confusion Criticism Dejection Embittered	Over-thinking Overly-concerned Sulk Suspicion Troubled Worthlessness	Acceptance Clever Contentedness Flexible Focused Hope	Mulling over Self-respect Serene Sweetness in life Thinking Tranquility
Grief	Bereavement Betrayed Blame Control Envy Gloom	Guilt Heartache/ Heartbroken Inconsolable Jealous Resentment Shamed (Toxic Shame)	Awareness Compassion Confident Courage Embracing Embracing life	Honorable Let go Mellow Release Responsive Strong
Fear	Afraid Anxiety (from fear) Frantic Insecure Jitters Nervous	Panic Scared Secretive Skeptical Uneasy Wishy-washy	Assurance Calm Centered Coherence Free Grounded	Restful Reverence Safe Secure Stillness Unlimited

The God Session

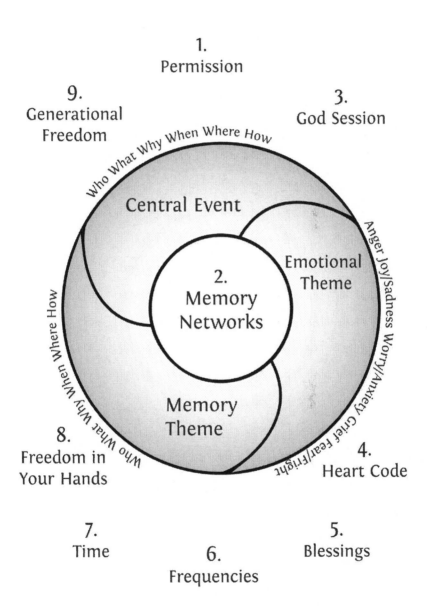

1.
Permission

9.
Generational
Freedom

3.
God Session

Who What Why When Where How

Central Event

Emotional
Theme

2.
Memory
Networks

Anger Joy/Sadness Worry/Anxiety Grief Fear/Fright

Memory
Theme

Who What Why When Where How

8.
Freedom in
Your Hands

4.
Heart Code

7.
Time

6.
Frequencies

5.
Blessings

1.

Permission

Self	Spirit
Others	Mind/Will/Emotions
God	Body

2.

Central Event
One memory that more than one person participated in. Each person may be affected in a different way.

Memory Theme
Many memories that all seem to be part of a common theme.

Emotional Theme
Memories that share a common or similar emotion. One emotion may have several variations.

Memory Network
Each person in your life fulfills at least one role. They are like spheres of influence that rotate around you and impact various areas of your life. A single person play the roles of confidant, friend, lover, spouse. In family businesses, that same person may also be your boss or supervisor. Each person's wounds will have a unique impact on how they fulfill that role and how they interact with you.

3.

God Session
-Come to the Throne boldly but honestly
-Non-judgment (toward yourself or others)
-Make your request (best outcome for all involved)
-Let go of the outcome
"Here you go, God. I'm going to let you take care of this."

4.

Heart Code
Truth, Trust, Clarity, Love – Accepting someone exactly the way they are without question, without reservation, without judgment. *"I can operate in truth, trust, clarity, and love, which brings health to my heart and healing to my soul. Bringing health and coherence to my heart allows me to walk in a measure of health that is unsurpassed."*

5.

Blessings
The heart's field surrounds the body and penetrates all the cells all the way into the DNA. Human intention influences DNA and affects not only you but those around you. Choose blessings. Choose life. Nurture all aspects of yourself and others.
Dimensional Aspects - Spirit, Mind/Will/Emotions, Soul, Body

6.

Frequencies
Spoken Words / Unspoken Thoughts
Words are audible sound. Thoughts are inaudible sound. Sound goes out in a ball and surrounds the body like the heart's field. Sound is frequency. Frequencies can build or destroy. Frequencies penetrate all the cells into the DNA. Frequencies also program water including the water that surrounds and bathes every cell. Surround yourself with words and thoughts that build and nurture.
May my spoken words and my unspoken thoughts be pleasing in Your sight. (Psalm 19:14)

7.

Time
Chronos – Chronological time
Kairos time – moments
We live in Kairos time. We live in the moment. We are interconnected / entangled through the Kairos Moments of memories. Bring all the Kairos moments together into one big Kairos Ball. Allow the memory to clear (to be healed) through all time and all space via the Kairos Ball.

8.

Freedom in Your Hands
Let go of worry and fear Let others have their own process
Create a space or ask God to create a space for you and for others to heal. Create a space filled with blessings and with positive, nurturing words, thoughts, and emotions.

9.

Generational Freedom
Clear memories, traits, emotions through all the generations. Did you inherit this _____? From whom?
Inheritance comes from many sources
- Birth (blood line)
- Adoption
  - Adopted family
  - Friends who are like family
- Teachers / Mentors
- Churches and other organizations to which you belong

Download the Free Bonus Materials!

Success is easier when you do the exercises on your own worksheets. By using these bonus materials, you can make your own notes and follow along step-by-step throughout each section of the book. Feel free to take these materials along with you so you have them whenever you need them.

Go to www.KathrynSpringman.com to download your free copy!

About the Author

Kathryn Springman loves all things creative! Her grandmother taught her to sew and taught her to use her imagination and use it well, always asking, "Can you imagine it this way or that? Can you imagine what something looks like in a different fabric or in a different color?" Her grandmother also encouraged her to look at the miraculous nature of life that surrounds all of us—in birdsong, in water flowing through a creek and the breeze in our hair.

Her mother taught her a love of puzzles and the wonder of how pieces go together to make the full picture (even if we can't see it). Her father provided her with the opportunity to witness the greatness of a pioneer healer whose bedside manner both calms and reassures.

Ms. Springman has over 30 years experience in prayer, intercession, and spiritual warfare. When a friend urged her to rethink and redefine health, this catapulted her into BodyTalk and alternative energy healing.

As an Advanced Certified and PaRama BodyTalk Practitioner and BodyTalk Access Trainer, she has continued to develop and expand techniques and offers consultations and conducts seminars to other practitioners regarding her techniques. In addition to teaching the BodyTalk Access for laypeople, she is working on a series of seminars for teaching laypeople her techniques.

Kathryn Springman brings new insights based on science and the ancient wisdom of God. Health is more than what we see in the body, and if we are struggling in the health of even one area of our lives—spiritually, mentally, emotionally, or physically—then on some level we are struggling with the health of all. Ms. Springman's approach to health is one that balances all those aspects of our being.

Ms. Springman has a full time BodyTalk practice in Edmond, Oklahoma where she conducts both in person and distance healing sessions. You can find her at:

Clinic website: www.okBodyTalk.com

Author website: www.KathrynSpringman.com

Facebook: www.FaceBook.com/kaspringman